18oct05

THE TWO

CW00811776

The Two Oceans

The Dark and the Light

by

Joanna Kirkby

With best wishes from
Joanna

William Sessions Limited
York, England

© Joanna Kirkby 2001

ISBN 1 85072 266 8

Printed from Author's disk
in 10½ on 11½ point Plantin Tyepface
by Sessions of York
The Ebor Press
York, England

CONTENTS

FOREWORD

IT IS DIFFICULT to give adequate thanks to the many who have discussed this subject with me and have given encouragement, helpful suggestions and advice. In particular I wish to thank Dr Geoffrey Nuttall for the time and care he has given to me on this project. His advice and scholarly criticism have been invaluable and have no doubt saved me from making blunders of a historical and theological nature particularly in my writing of the events, personalities and beliefs of the seventeenth century. I should also like to thank Christina Lawson and her successor Mary Jo Clogg, Librarians of Woodbrooke Library, also Malcolm Thomas and the staff of Friends House library who were all patient and helpful in locating books for me. There are so many who have encouraged me along the way, too great a number to mention each one personally; I thank Mollie Hooper (formerly Mollie Grubb) for her help in the early days. My thanks also to Vera Massey and to my sister Phyllis Short for their constructive criticism. Penny Robinson has typed the manuscript and I could not have done without her encouraging and skilled help.

I owe a debt to my cousin Joseph Brayshaw and my husband Michael Kirkby (both now departed this life) who as dedicated genealogists did much of the research on which my writing of our seventeenth century forebears is based. My brother Henry Rodwell wrote of his own experiences in the wartime FAU China Convoy, and of our parents' lives in China in his book *China Mission* and I have incorporated some of this material here.

Those who already know something of the conditions of life in the seventeenth century and the rise of the Quakers may wish to skip the Introduction and pass directly to later chapters. Those looking for a more academic account have many other books on Quaker theology and history from which to choose.

INTRODUCTION

QUAKERS have always held a belief in the Inner Light or Inward Christ and have written and spoken of this since our beginnings as a religious movement. We have rarely given consideration in our writings or discussions to the Inner Dark - human wickedness, the evil of some motives and actions. "Wickedness" and "evil" I define as any conscious or unconscious thought or action which leads to the treating of anyone as not a neighbour but "other", which then allows us to do them harm. A group of people who together are bent on doing harm can do far more than they could as individuals. Evil can also result from, for example, the worship (i.e. "giving highest worth to") of self-aggrandisement, of the amassing of possessions, of the desire to dominate, and from spiritual pride, the 'hubris' of our age.

As I have learned more of early Friends and the persecution and cruel treatment which they often received, I want to know how they coped? How did they respond to what both Paul in the first century and George Fox in the seventeenth described as "the Powers of Darkness"? How did they experience and deal with their own Inner Dark? Were they victorious in their struggles? If so, what can we learn from them? What of succeeding Quaker generations who have faced different darkness? And how do twenty first century Quakers react today?

Some years ago I started to write on the subject of the Inner Light and the Inner and Outer Dark as Quakers perceived these, from the seventeenth century to the twentieth. I began with Paul and Augustine, followed by the views of Luther and Calvin and the seventeenth century Quakers' rejection of "crying up sin". Fox's theme was the possibility of the overcoming of sin and evil in this world, for early Friends held to the positive belief that the victory was to be gained by the opening up of the heart to the Spirit of the Inward Christ and obedience to that Light within. George Fox described in his great "opening", how he saw "that there was an ocean of darkness and death, but an infinite ocean of light and love, which flowed over the ocean of darkness".

My attempt to examine such a theme through the centuries, proved to be a much bigger task than I had imagined and as Dr Geoffrey Nuttall commented to me, the resultant book was becoming just another history of the Society of Friends, of which there are many already by authors better qualified than I feel myself to be. So I dropped this project, or thought that I had, but at some interior level the interest, even "concern" to delve into this aspect of Quakerism did not leave me. Janey O'Shea, when Quaker Studies Tutor at Woodbrooke recognised this and encouraged me to write in a more personal way. This I have now tried to do, using as illustration, in Part 1, experiences in the lives of my family, my Quaker forebears and some other Quaker connections; and in Part 2, my own upbringing and life as a Quaker, with some general comments on the Society of Friends.

PART ONE: THE PAST

SEVENTEENTH-CENTURY BACKGROUND

LOOKING BACK to the time of the beginning of the Quaker movement in the seventeenth century, we see a country where most people were occupied in farming or local small industries and crafts, so that villages and towns were virtually self-sufficient. There were cities, some of middling-size such as Bristol or Norwich, with London much the largest, but these are hardly recognisable as cities in comparison with ours today. There were traders and merchants but overall, Britain was mainly a rural economy. Do we imagine a "Merrie England", an idyll of productive land, bright and clear streams, meadows full of wild-flowers and birdsong and happy folk living a healthy, hard-working life on the land, enjoying hay-making and "harvest-home" feasts with singing and dancing? We may recall that many such customs disappeared during the sober and austere times of the Puritans, but also that such bucolic traditions persisted into the nineteenth century as is shown in the novels of Thomas Hardy. Life for many in the seventeenth century was "nasty, brutish and short", specially at times of severe weather, harvest failure and disease, with plague a recurrent feature. During the Civil Wars many men died, some suffered greatly from wounds or disablement and all the population suffered from the accompanying shortages of the necessities of life. Even in times of peace there was a high mortality rate, especially for women at childbirth and for babies and young children. In addition there was a spirit of intolerance which fostered both political and religious persecution. Recently I visited Harvington Hall in Worcestershire, one of the centres of Roman Catholicism in the locality. There are several priest-holes in the house and a well-disguised chapel for the celebration of the Mass. All Roman Catholics were treated extremely harshly at this time, particularly the priests when dragged from their hiding-places. As late as 1679, Father Thomas Wall was sent to Worcester, there to be hung, drawn and quartered in front of a large crowd. Joseph Besse described in his *Sufferings of the People called Quakers* how many early Friends were persecuted, imprisoned and ill-treated, but none were put to death in so barbarous a manner: barbarous in our view today but not to everyone in the past. During George Fox's lifetime violence in many spheres of life was taken for granted, not only against those of the "wrong" political or religious belief.

It was quite legal for men to beat their wives and children, masters to beat their apprentices and for women suspected of witchcraft to be ill-used and sometimes executed. Many judicial punishments were cruel and degrading; the pillory was a common sight, as was whipping at the cart's end, even flogging to near death. Imprisonment was in vile conditions where gaolers were often brutal, and many prisoners sickened and died.

For some, the events of the Civil Wars (1642-1651) were of major importance in their lives, their thinking, their religious beliefs and later actions being profoundly influenced. This is somewhat difficult to bear in mind because Fox and other Quaker writers hardly mention the Civil Wars themselves. Yet there were battles during the 1640s in the East Midlands, George Fox's home territory, and in 1651 the armies were engaged in fighting through Cumberland and Lancashire, the area considered "the cradle of Quakerism". The Civil Wars were especially ferocious, for families were divided, brother fought against brother and father against son. The weapons of the time, such as the pike, the pole-axe and the sword were used for the amputation of limbs, for decapitation and disembowelment. Atrocities were committed on both sides, as in all wars: towns were besieged and sacked, homes burnt, women raped, farms pillaged. Some who later joined the Quaker movement, had fought in these bloody contests, for example, James Nayler, so great an inspiration to the early Quaker movement, had been for many years a soldier in the Parliamentary army. He had fought at the Battle of Dunbar, a battle in which there was a terrible slaughter of the Royalists. Modern historical research has shown that greater areas of the country were affected than previously thought. Wherever the armies needed food, fodder, horses or quarters for themselves the local population suffered. Many must have shared Edward Burrough's despair,

> "For when we looked abroad and beheld the world, behold it was altogether darkness, and even as a wilderness, and desolate and barren of good fruit".

3

In reading of the background and experience of our Quaker fore-bears, we can gain some insight into their world. We need also a leap of imaginative understanding to enter into the lives of those of a period so very different from our own. Their concepts of good and evil were based on the Bible which they knew intimately; George Fox was said to know the whole Bible by heart. Their upbringing and lives were centred on religion at a depth almost unknown in our country today (except among for example, the Moslems). For most people of the seventeenth century this religious training was Calvinist, which meant that they believed that only the "elect", the chosen of God, would reach heaven after death, all others without conversion and baptism being considered "reprobate", would be damned to hell and torment. The doctrine of the "Fall" in the Garden of Eden and therefore "Original Sin" was accepted by Protestants and Catholics alike. Calvin went so far as to claim that man

> "neither knows, desires nor undertakes anything that is not wicked, perverse, iniquitous and defiled".

Is it any wonder that many felt despair at what they saw around them, as Burroughs expressed so strongly, and that many had also a deep sense of their wrongdoing in this life and fearfulness about the next? What a relief, what a revelation to hear Fox or Nayler or Margaret Fell or other Quaker leaders giving the gloriously positive message that men and women too, and even children could by following the Inner Light, the Inward Christ, be restored to the state of innocence of Adam and Eve before the "Fall". And how wonderful for the women of that time to be included in the promise of such a blessed state! So, rather than "election" or "reprobation", the watch-words of the Children of Light or Friends of Truth (as the first Quakers called themselves) were "restoration" and "regeneration". Nevertheless they felt the "Powers of Darkness" were very strong and identified with the apostle Paul who wrote in Ephesians Ch6v12 (Authorised Version).

> "we wrestle not against flesh and blood, but against principali-ties, against powers, against the rulers of the darkness of this world, against spiritual wickedness in high places".

They believed all injustice, oppression, lying and dishonesty were the work of the devil, as were any actions which were contrary to the teachings of Jesus as given in the Gospels. Therefore, both swearing and the taking of solemn oaths was wrong and forbidden to the Friends, the true followers of Jesus, as was the payment of tithes to maintain the "hireling priests" and "steeple-houses" of an apostate church.

4

They slowly came to see that fighting with "carnal weapons" was to be replaced by a spiritual war using spiritual weapons by "putting on the whole armour of God". They knew that Christ had come again and would give his faithful ones the victory in the war between good and evil, between the Light and the "Powers of Darkness". They believed that the Children of Light would by the power of the Inward Christ and in the purposes of God, usher in the New Jerusalem, the peaceable kingdom, where righteousness, justice, true goodness and above all, love would reign. Many Quakers believed, with other radical religious groups, that they were living in the "end-times" prophesied in the "Book of Revelations". This was to be the time of the "Lamb's War": Jesus, the Lamb of God, the Light of the world, against Satan, the Prince of Darkness of this "World". The "World" in this sense meant all wickedness, all greed, cruelty and vanity, the social divisions in a hierarchical society, the unjust persecuting state and the persecuting churches, whether Protestant or Roman Catholic. And if, as soldiers in the "Lamb's War" they were forced to suffer, then by the power of the Spirit, they would be given strength to suffer in following Jesus and they would win through.

Again the words of Paul spoke to them in the Epistle to the Romans:

> "Who shall separate us from the love of Christ? Shall tribulation, or distress, or persecution, or famine, or nakedness, or peril, or sword? ... Nay, in all these things we are more than conquerors through him that loved us." Romans Ch8v35 and v37 (Authorised Version).

Friends did indeed suffer as we learn from many sources; and many bore their suffering courageously; many endured and many won through. Some however, found it all too much for them and "fell away"; some fled the country and a large number of Friends compromised by signing a statement of belief so that they would be included in the proposed Toleration Act of 1689.

George Fox and Margaret Fell in their writing and preaching took the idea of the victory of Light over Darkness even further. Since Christ was Light, and there was no darkness in him : therefore, there would be no darkness in those who walked in obedience to the Light. Thus they taught that perfection in this life was attainable by both men and women. This was an extremely attractive teaching, particularly to women of the time, who were not even considered by some theologians to have souls to be saved. This was an extreme and over-optimistic view of human nature, and Friends had very soon indeed, to face their imperfection, even failures. In the late 1650s there was the sad case of James Nayler (1634-1656) who had been as prominent a leader of the Friends as George Fox himself. W.C. Braithwaite in his history of the early Quakers concluded that Quakerism

> "after Nayler's Fall ... abated its high language about personal infallibility" and became more aware "of the dangers that attended enthusiasm".

The over-enthusiasm of some of Nayler's followers when they welcomed his ride on horseback into Bristol as though it was an enactment of Jesus' triumphal entry into Jerusalem, led to a charge of blasphemy. This was considered so serious a matter that it was referred to Parliament, with the result that James Nayler was imprisoned, pilloried, his tongue bored with a hot iron and his forehead branded with the letter "B". These measures were followed by a further period of imprisonment in solitary confinement. Throughout he maintained his dignity and bore his sufferings with humility and fortitude; in Christ-like spirit he was able to forgive his torturers as did Jesus on the cross.

Darkness had fallen indeed, not only on Nayler as a leader, but on the Quakers of the time who aroused increased hostility and were reviled for this aberration in one of their chief proponents. A wonderful inflowing of the light over this darkness came to Nayler before his death a short time after his release from prison. He was reconciled to Friends and in his dying words gave this testimony.

> "There is a spirit which I feel that delights to do no evil, nor avenge any wrong, but delights to endure all things, in hope to enjoy its own in the end. Its hope is to outlive all wrath and contention, and to weary out all exaltation and cruelty, or what-ever is of a nature contrary to itself. It sees to the end of all temptations. As it bears no evil in itself, so it conceives none in thoughts to any other. If it is betrayed, it bears it, for its ground and spring is the mercies and forgiveness of God. Its crown is meekness, its life is everlasting love unfeigned; it takes its kingdom with entreaty and not with contention and keeps it with lowliness of mind." Quaker Faith and Practice (19.12)

How did early, persecuted Friends cope with their own reactions? Some, like James Nayler reported an inflowing of love towards others, even towards those who ill-used them. Yet others were so totally involved in defending and preaching their new-found faith and in caring for their families in times of persecution that all their energies were thus absorbed.

A good deal of any anger they felt was expressed in public disputations or in the writing of tracts to support their own beliefs and to attack those with whom they disagreed. The language they used was intemperate, even virulent and vituperative rather than "Quakerly" in our modern view. They took seriously the words of the Bible

"'Vengeance is mine, I will repay' saith the Lord". Romans (Ch12v19)

So they did not seek to revenge themselves on those who treated them so badly but believed implicitly that God was a just God and would punish all wrongdoers on their behalf. Fox's "Journal" lists numbers of persecutors of Quakers who came to grief, and there is barely hidden satisfaction at this outcome. One example will suffice: my husband's Kirkby family were from Yorkshire but had distant relatives across to the West in Furness in Lancashire. Col. Richard Kirkby was a local magistrate and hounded George Fox whenever he came into Lancashire, imprisoning him on several occasions in shocking conditions. At last in 1666, Fox reported in his "Journal" that "Colonel Kirkby wasted away all his estate and buried three wives". This was believed by Fox and other Friends to be God's way of dealing with the wicked, who walked not in the Light, but in darkness.

SEVENTEENTH CENTURY BACKGROUND

Geoffrey Nuttall: F.D. Maurice Lecture 1958, *Christianity and Violence.*

P.R. Newman: *Atlas of the Civil War* (Map 42), Macmillan, New York, 1985.

Ibid.; (Map 49).

Taylor Downing & Maggie Millman: *The Civil War*, Parkgate 1998 (Channel Four)

Edward Burrough: Introduction to *The Great Mystery* by George Fox, *An Epistle to the Reader*, New Foundation George Fox Fund Inc. State College, Pennsylvania, USA.

John Calvin: *Institutes of the Christian Religion II*, chap. 2, vol. xx of the Library of Christian Classics, SCM Press MCMLV.

Joseph Besse: *A Collection of the Sufferings of the People called Quakers 1650-1689*, London 1953.

William C. Braithwaite: *The Beginnings of Quakerism*, 1981, Cambridge University Press/William Sessions, York.

Ibid.: *The Second Period of Quakerism*, 1979, Sessions, York.

Leo Damrosch: *The Sorrows of the Quaker Jesus*, Harvard University Press, Cambridge USA & London 1996.

Quaker Faith & Practice 1994, (Extract 19.12).

GENERAL BOOKS CONSULTED

Hugh Barbour: *The Quakers in Puritan England*, New Haven & London, Yale University Press, 1964.

Ed. Hugh Barbour & A.O. Roberts: *Early Quaker Writings*, 1973. William B. Eerdmans Publishing Co., Michigan, USA.

A. Neave Brayshaw: *The Quakers, their Story and Message*, 1946, 4th Impression, George Allen & Unwin Ltd. and Sessions of York, 1982.

Matthew Fox: *Original Blessing*, Bear & Co., Santa Fe, New Mexico, 1983.

Douglas Gwyn: *Apocalypse of the Word*, Friends United Press, Richmond, Indiana, USA, 1984.

Christopher Hill: *The World Turned Upside Down; radical ideas in the English Revolution*, Penguin Books, 1975.

Barry Ingle: *First Among Friends, George Fox and the Creation of Quakerism*, Oxford University Press, 1994.

Ed. Michael Mullet: *New Light on George Fox*, Sessions, York, 1991.

Geoffrey Nuttall: *The Holy Spirit in Puritan Faith & Experience*, University of Chicago Press, rep. 1992.

John Punshon: *Portrait in Grey*, Quaker Home Service, London, 1984.

Barry Reay: *Quakers and the English Revolution*, Temple Smith, 1985.

Ed. Cecil W. Sharman: *No more but my Love*. Letters of George Fox, Quaker Home Service, 1980.

CHAPTER 1

"IN THE LIFE"

NOW I want to look at the lives of some seventeenth-century Quakers to try to see how their Quaker beliefs worked out in practice. Did they truly find that in turning to the Inward Christ they were so filled with a sense of joy and love, that they were enabled to endure their suffering in a good spirit without bitterness and rancour? Did "walking in the Light" empower them spiritually against the "Powers of Darkness"? Did they find that "the darkness is passing away and the true light already shineth" as promised in the first letter of John (Ch2Vol8)? These are some of the questions I have asked myself when reading of the lives of my Quaker forebears.

On my mother's side there are Quakers back to the 1660s, when our direct ancestors, Charles and Elizabeth Lloyd joined "the Friends of Truth". The Lloyds of Dolobran in Montgomery, mid-Wales, came of long lines of distinguished land-owning families. Charles and Elizabeth (née Stanley) had three sons, the eldest, another Charles (b. 1637) followed by Thomas, both of whom became Quakers in adult life whereas the third son, John, joined the "establishment" as a Chancery clerk. In 1657 when the eldest Charles, was only nineteen years old, his father died and he was recalled from Oxford to run the considerable family estate of Dolobran in mid-Wales.

It was of prime importance in those troubled times that Charles should have both a wife and an heir. He was obviously a very eligible young bachelor and could have chosen a wife from one of the neighbouring families. Instead he chose to ride on horseback some days' journey to the West of Pembrokeshire. There at Stackpole and East Moor the Lort family owned a great deal of land and were described as living in feudal splendour. They were Independent in religion, but at times had supported the King; in spite of this, the Lorts had accepted high office under the Commonwealth. Probably the Lorts considered themselves of a higher rank and therefore socially superior to the Lloyds, a matter of importance in those times. Nevertheless, Charles wooed and won the hand of Elizabeth Lort. Perhaps this is not so surprising since Charles Lloyd had an honourable Welsh pedigree on his father's side and his mother was a Stanley. In later years his own son wrote of him:

> "Charles Lloyd was in his person handsome, comely and portly, rather tall than of middle stature, personable every way, of a fresh lively countenance, generally cheerful and pleasant".

They must have made an attractive couple for there are contemporary references to Elizabeth's good looks, "fine clothes" delicate nature and "stately bearing". Charles Lloyd and Elizabeth Lort were married in Stackpole Elidor Church in 1662.

The next year was a momentous one for them both, for their first child was born at Dolobran and also named Charles. Only a month later this child's father was in Welshpool prison for conscience sake, for he had allied himself with the despised and feared Quakers. Lord Herbert had committed him with others to Welshpool gaol on the grounds that they had been present at a gathering forbidden by law, in this case a Quaker meeting in Charles Lloyd's house, Dolobran Hall, and that he and the others arrested had refused to swear the Oath of Allegiance. Thus these Quakers and their sympathisers suffered for being faithful to their new-found religious convictions.

Charles wrote to his brother Thomas from Welshpool Gaol:

> "This is a nasty place and the gaoler but a cruel man in his usage of us".

"Nasty" is hardly a strong enough adjective to describe the place in which Charles Lloyd with three other men and also three women were imprisoned. Welshpool gaol was a two-storey building, the upper storey where the "rogues and villains" were confined while the room below them (approximately 15ft by 12ft) held the Quakers, who were considered to be a threat to both church and state. The gaoler would not allow his Quaker prisoners to have visitors nor to receive the food and bedding which friends and relatives sent in for them. Worse still, the floor boarding above them was ill-fitting, with gaps, and as Richard Davies has recorded:

> "the felons and malefactors in a chamber being overhead their chamber-pots and excrement etc often falling upon them. Charles Lloyd, who was a little before in Commission of the

Peace, was put in a little smoky room, and did lie upon straw for a considerable time".

Not only was Charles Lloyd a Commissioner of the Peace but he had recently been nominated as High Sheriff of the county of Montgomery. His imprisonment in such conditions was hard for him to bear, but it caused consternation to his family and to the gentry of the neighbourhood, with condemnation from some and at first, little sympathy from his wife of less than a year. Charles had periods of ill-health for the rest of his life, but was more fortunate than two of his fellow prisoners who died through the foul conditions. In fact, being committed to prison was a death penalty for over 300 out of a total of about 1,200 Friends imprisoned between the Restoration of Charles the Second and the Toleration Act of 1689.

George Fox had faith that if he suffered prison in a Christian spirit, his suffering would bring others to follow the Inward Light of Christ. We are not told if the Lloyds suffered imprisonment and loss in the same hope, but this is very likely. Suffering for the Truth was part of the duty of a soldier in the Lamb's War against what Paul described as "the powers of darkness". If I put myself in their shoes, I imagine I would experience righteous indignation at the unjust treatment; I might well feel great anger towards my persecutors and towards the informers who received money to make things worse for me and mine. Nevertheless, there is no hint of these negative emotions in the records we have; in fact Charles Lloyd's son was able to say of him after his death, (in 1698) that he hated no-one, but hated only evil. Fox claimed it was possible for the true follower of Jesus Christ to get "atop of sin" through the empowering of the Spirit; and this teaching is in some way similar to the modern psychological idea of the possibility of "sublimation". Maybe it was less difficult for early Friends because, like the persecuted early Christians, they believed that the Spirit of Christ was come to them and that the "Kingdom of God is nigh".

When Charles had been in prison for about six months a small miracle occurred. His wife, brought up in happy circumstances, with the comfort given by wealth, voluntarily joined her young husband, taking baby Charles with her. She must have loved him deeply for she did not as yet share his religious faith but

"was made willing to lie upon straw with her dear and tender husband".

The baby ceased to thrive in this environment so was put out to nurse with a woman who lived near enough for Elizabeth to visit him frequently, as she was not forced to remain within the prison.

Things continued in this way for some time, Elizabeth chafing, since she did not understand what made her husband cling so obstinately to such extreme views. And how insulting to her must have seemed the behaviour of the Dolobran servants who had become Quaker with their master and addressed everybody with "thee" and "thou" instead of the "you" which was customary in speaking to a social superior like herself! The gaoler meanwhile had been persuaded to allow the little family the use of a small house in Welshpool, only a short distance from the prison, which was a blessing to Elizabeth particularly as she was again pregnant. This child when born, was named Sampson, a Lort family name, and he was the direct Lloyd ancestor of my family. Before the time of his birth, Charles must have felt greatly encouraged, for they were allowed some visitors. These were Margaret Fell (whose second husband was George Fox) and one of her daughters, who were travelling in Wales to bring practical help and words of power and comfort to persecuted Friends. Now Elizabeth was able to meet and talk with and question "the mother of Quakerism", a person of similar rank and upbringing as herself. So Elizabeth took Margaret Fell and her daughter Sarah, from house-prison in Welshpool to Dolobran Hall where they could be entertained in a suitable fashion. In answer most probably to her hostess' questions Margaret Fell related her own "convincement" of the Truth through the preaching of George Fox. Her then husband Judge Fell was satisfied that the Quakers were no danger to the state and were sincere God-fearing people, leading virtuous lives. Although he never joined "the Friends of Truth" himself, he protected them and supported his wife in the making of their home, Swarthmoor Hall, a centre for the growing Quaker movement. At Dolobran Margaret was able to speak from the heart to Elizabeth Lloyd and direct her to the "Inner Light of Christ", the "Inward Teacher" instead of following the teachings of this or that religious leader or preacher. Elizabeth had been brought up as an Independent, in a faith based on Calvinist doctrines where the Bible, the Word of God was the only authority, and the "elect" alone, those chosen and predestined by God would be saved from damnation in the everlasting fires of Hell. To learn that Friends believed in a "Universal saving Light" and that Christ was the Word of God, the Scriptures were but the words of God, was at total variance.

Early Friends hardly ever spoke or wrote of Hell or eternal damnation. Margaret Fell's deep faith and her sincerity must have touched Elizabeth's heart and at last her husband's faith began to make sense to her. Since women had so inferior a status in the prevalent Protestantism of the time it was astonishing to learn that Friends believed not only that women had souls, but that they were permitted to minister and to pray in public meetings for worship, which was a thing unheard of in the mainstream churches. George Fox and Margaret Fell were prominent in teaching that men and women who joined the "Children of Light", the Quakers, would be restored to the condition of Adam and Eve before the "Fall" as described in Genesis and were therefore "helpmeets", and spiritually equal before God and people alike. There was no hint in Quaker teaching that women were temptresses, part of the "Powers of Darkness" as some theologians and early Church fathers feared. Fox himself spoke and wrote many times that "marriage was an honourable state", and children born from sexual union were born not with original sin but each one a child of God created in his image. What a contrast to the teaching of Augustine, followed to some extent by the Protestant reformers, that each one is an inheritor of the sin of Adam, and that this "Original Sin" was passed from one generation on to the next by the act of sexual intercourse! No doubt all these aspects of Quaker teaching influenced Elizabeth, but the faith of her husband, the words and spirit of Margaret Fell and the strong impression made by her fellow prisoners' endurance of their suffering brought Elizabeth to the Quaker faith. For Charles this was great encouragement, an answer to prayer and a cause of thankfulness that he and his wife were now united at the deepest level, their shared religious faith.

Charles and Elizabeth Lloyd were imprisoned for twelve years, for a few years in Welshpool Gaol, for most of the time in the small house on the outskirts of the town where they had been given permission to live with their children. When eventually they were able to return to Dolobran Hall, they found the house in a poor state, the farm short of cattle which had been driven away. Year by year the Lloyds were fined for non-attendance at church, the holding of meetings of worship which was against the law, and for not paying tithes to the priest of Meifod Church. Joseph Besse writes of the:

> "trials, afflictions and sufferings, cruel mockings and scourgings, bonds imprisonments and deaths, which this religious people underwent for the exercise of a good conscience during

a violent storm of persecution of nearly forty years continuance".

How did Charles and Elizabeth endure? How did they have the inner strength to suffer so much? How did they cope with the natural human responses of indignation and anger over their harsh treatment and the injustice done to their family? Yet they did endure and they somehow were able to see their persecutors as having "that of God" within them. Charles wrote to his brother Thomas when he was imprisoned in Welshpool:

"I am in gaol, yet peace and gladness are in my heart and I can praise Him that hath counted me worthy to suffer for his name".

On several occasions Charles had the opportunity to sue for wrongful arrest and for assault, but this he did not do. Charles himself wrote of the experience of his first meeting for worship which was held in the house of one of his tenants:

"The Lord was not wanting - but afforded unto us his good presence, and the Word was with power so that it reached unto our hearts and understanding."

Charles and Elizabeth were changed indeed. After joining with "The Friends of Truth", they behaved very differently. All were to be addressed as "thee" and "thou" whatever their social status; Charles would no longer remove his hat nor "bow and scrape" to his social superiors. They lived more simply on their return to Dolobran: and Charles and Thomas Lloyd risked much as they "travelled in the Ministry" as Friends. They were no longer chiefly occupied with the pleasures and duties of their class.

CHAPTER 2

WITNESS: THE 17th-CENTURY QUAKER RESPONSE TO INNER AND OUTER DARK

W E ARE TOLD by biologists that animals faced with danger either fight or take flight. This seems to be as true of human beings, though they can choose to fight not with "carnal weapons", that is by a physical response, but with spiritual weapons. This understanding, that the fight was to be fought with spiritual weapons came hard and slowly to those who had joined with the Friends after having been in the Civil wars, which they had hoped would bring in the Kingdom of God. And had not Fox himself in his early ministry advocated the sending of an army against the Pope in Rome? As has been described, being a spiritual soldier in the Lamb's War included willingness to suffer and endure long years of persecution. For some this proved to be just too much and they gave up the struggle and fled the fight by disassociating themselves from Friends. Others, perhaps 5,000 from Wales during the period of the most severe persecution of the Welsh Quakers, took up William Penn's offer to flee the country for a new life in his colony of Pennsylvania. In spite of pleas from the Yearly Meeting in Wales, Friends continued to leave for sanctuary in America, where in 1682 the "Welsh Tract" was purchased from Penn. Thomas Lloyd, after many years of imprisonment and harassment, with his wife and large family emigrated to Pennsylvania, where he eventually became William Penn's Deputy. His elder brother Charles, on the other hand, bought land in Pennsylvania but never set sail to settle there. After release from prison he remained at Dolobran, running the estate, was a leading member of the little Quaker meeting there and gave his support to the much reduced numbers of Welsh Friends. His second son, Sampson, also left Wales, not to go across the sea to America but nearer home, to settle in Birmingham where Dissenters like Unitarians and Quakers were made welcome and were able to live in freedom.

If Friends did not flee, how did they fight? They endured, in the spirit of Christian discipleship; they took what action was open to them against the evils of injustice and oppression and ill-treatment. They took action in a manner familiar to future generations of Quakers; they fought the "Powers of Darkness" with courage and perseverance; they were non-violent resisters in keeping their meetings for worship, in refusing to pay tithes to an "apostate" church, in refusing to swear the Oath of Allegiance or to remove their hats in court. They visited those in authority and asked them for justice and better treatment, speaking as Fox said to their "inner witness", "answering that of God" even in the oppressor and tormentor, as much as in them lay. As far as possible they used the law of the land for their purposes. A good example is the use the Friends imprisoned at Welshpool made of the right to petition the newly restored King. Hardly had Charles Lloyd and his fellow Friends arrived in gaol than they signed a petition to the "Justices and Magistrates Of this County of Montgomery". They pointed out that the King had signed a Declaration of Indulgence on 26th December 1662 which promised freedom of conscience and that none should be punished for practising their faith provided that they lived peaceably. However this petition was ignored by the Justices who were no doubt Royalists with some scores to settle. Richard Davies and Thomas Lloyd then set out to see Lord Herbert who had committed the Friends to Welshpool gaol, and asked him for their release. Although he did not agree to set them at liberty, they learned that he had sent private instructions, which is probably the reason that Charles Lloyd was permitted to live in better conditions and eventually the gaoler treated all these Quaker prisoners with more leniency. In the meantime Richard Davies reports:

> "My friend Thomas Lloyd and I were moved to go and visit most of the justices that had a hand in committing friends to prison; we began at the farthest justice in Machynlleth,..."

The visits to suffering Friends and to the authorities, "speaking truth to power" were continued by Richard Davies and Thomas Lloyd for many years. Charles Lloyd was on parole while imprisoned and was able to join in this work. They approached Lord and Lady Powis and through Lord Hyde, petitioned the King. Their approaches to Lord Herbert must have touched his conscience for when an informer asked for a warrant against the Lloyds he refused, saying that it was enough that he had been obliged to obey the law by sending his neighbours to prison, without making things worse. For informers were handsomely rewarded with goods and property of those they informed against. Fox gives examples in his "Journal" of how his piercing truth and power gained the respect and sometimes the "convincement" of justices as well as gaolers.

After the Restoration, Friends, William Penn and Margaret Fell among them, were very active at the highest political level. Thomas Lloyd and others were instrumental in preventing the resurrection of the Act "De Heretico Comburendo", a narrow escape for Friends and other Dissenters. In 1672 the King suspended all Penal Laws against Non-conformists. The Quakers were sufficiently well-organised to take the Letters Patent signed by the King, by horse all over the country, so freeing from prison 491 Friends including Charles Lloyd. When the Lloyd family were back in Dolobran, Charles with Thomas and others continued their visits to Friends in prison in Wales, Bristol and the south west of the country. Wherever possible, they preached to any who would listen. On one memorable occasion Charles and Thomas were invited to a lengthy disputation with the Bishop of St Asaph. They argued that the established church was not set up in gospel order; after some hours of discourse the Bishop actually complimented the two Quakers on their presentation.

Things did not always go so smoothly, and the Welsh Friends were in trouble with Fox and other Quakers for following the leading of John Perrot who, on his return from imprisonment by the Inquisition in Italy gained quite a considerable following in Britain in the early 1660s. This was centred on the removal of the hat for prayer, but deeper issues were involved. Isaac Pennington and other prominent and deeply spiritual Friends also took John Perrot's part for some time before concluding that they had been led astray. Richard Davies gives an account of the influence of John Perrot and his followers in Wales in the so-called "hat controversy" commenting that:

> "In time the Lord broke in among them, and opened the understandings of some of them, and they began to reason among themselves, and saw that they were in darkness; so that most of them were restored again to their first love and loved and died faithful to truth ..."

Richard Davies himself, with Charles and Elizabeth Lloyd and fifteen other Friends signed a humble statement, repudiating their earlier stance:

> "We whose names are here under-written, are those that thou has been seeking to insinuate thy corrupt principles into; and also are those that testify against that seducing spirit that thou art gone into; and most of us do know the terror and judgement

of the Lord, for receiving that spirit ... and we have all seen the hurtful effects of that spirit, and in the fear of the Lord, we do deny the same ...".

And he went on to describe the effects of the reading of this signed letter at a later monthly meeting:

"where the Lord melted, tendered and mollified our hearts and caused us to praise the Lord, for his great goodness and mercy to us, in bringing us out of that darkness ... and friends were careful afterwards of receiving any spirit that might tend to the breach of love and unity among us".

William C Braithwaite in explaining John Perrot's position in his *Second Period of Quakerism*, sees him as a mystic who wanted as it were, pure spirit without body, therefore all practical arrangements, even for meeting at stated times and places were to be denied; each individual was to act by the guidance of the spirit as he or she felt personally led. He comments:

"The Perrot position ... had it been adopted, would have meant the rapid disintegration of the Quaker movement".

This issue of the conflict between the spirit and the "body" or structure supporting that spirit, the conflict between individual and corporate "leadings" did not go away.

Dolobran Meeting House. Built 1699.
BY COURTESY OF JACK WHITAKER

The 1990s are a time of individualism; have we now solved the problem of keeping a balance between the individual member's insights and wishes and those of the Society of Friends as a whole? We do well to ponder on the historical fact that the many religious movements of the seventeenth century such as the Muggletonians and the Ranters, who were completely individualistic in their understanding of their faith, have vanished. Only the well-organised Quakers, with their emphasis on corporate witness have survived into the twenty first century as the Society of Friends.

CHARLES & ELIZABETH LLOYD AND WITNESS OF 17TH CENTURY FRIENDS

Samuel Lloyd: *The Quaker Lloyds of Birmingham*, Cornish Bros., Birmingham, 1905.

Quoted by Humphrey Lloyd: *The Quaker Lloyds in the Industrial Revolution*, Hutchinson, London, 1975.

Richard Davies: *An Account of the Convincement, Exercises, Services and Travels of that Ancient Servant of the Lord, Richard Davies, with some Relation of Ancient Friends in the Spreading of the Truth in North Wales*, 4th edition, James Phillips, London, 1790.

James Besse: *A Collection of the Sufferings of the People called Quakers from 1650-1689*, taken from original records and other authentic accounts by Joseph Besse, London, 1753. (Note: Besse's calculation of those Quakers who died in prison is not accepted by some later scholars.)

GENERAL BOOKS CONSULTED

William Gregory Morris, compiler of *John Ap John and Early Records of Friends in Wales"*, 1907 ed. by Norman Penney for the Friends Historical Society, London Headley Bros.

Anna Lloyd Braithwaite Thomas: *The Quaker Seekers in Wales*, 1924, The Swarthmore Press, London.

Rev. T. Mardy Rees: *A History of the Quakers in Wales*, W. Spurrell & Sons, Carmarthen, 1925.

Isabel Ross: *Margaret Fell, Mother of Quakerism*, Longmans, London, reprinted Sessions, York, 1984.

CHAPTER 3

JOHN BELLERS 1654-1725

FRIENDS emphasised, from their earliest days, that their faith in God, their love of God, must lead also to love of neighbours, as Jesus himself commanded. The Epistle of James (ch2vv14-18) was much quoted:

> "What doth it profit, my brethren, though a man say he hath faith, and have not works? Can faith save him? If a brother or sister be naked, and destitute of daily food, And one of you say unto them, Depart in peace, be ye warmed and filled; notwith-standing ye gave them not those things which are needful to the body; what doth it profit? Even so, faith, if it hath not works, is dead, being alone. Yea, a man may say, Thou hast faith, And I have works: shew me thy faith without thy works, and I will shew thee my faith by my works."

During the years of persecution, Friends set up Meeting for Sufferings and 'boxes' to care for their own distressed members and their families; they had little energy or opportunity to take action on behalf of the poor and oppressed in society in general. Nevertheless George Fox and others exhorted magistrates and those in authority to take steps to deal with the injustices and social problems of the day. As William Penn said:

> "True godliness don't turn men out of the world but enables them to live better in it and excites their endeavours to mend it".

Social reform has always been on the agenda as a paramount duty for all Christians. In John Bellers, who lived from the middle of the seventeenth century to the end of the first quarter of the eighteenth, the Society of Friends had a most remarkable social reformer, a pioneer and practical prophet. He was praised and emulated many years after his death by the great Robert Owen, who acknowledged his debt to

Bellers' practical ideals. Karl Marx wrote of him in *Das Kapital* that John Bellers was "a veritable phenomenon in the history of political economy". And yet his life and "Proposals" for the amelioration of many social evils have been largely forgotten, even among Friends.

As a young man growing up in London, he had seen the often despairing lot of the "labouring classes" and of the paupers who formed the bottom layer of the hierarchical social pyramid. John Bellers was himself imprisoned briefly as a Quaker, and from the experience of imprisonment he was the more understanding of the problems of poverty and unemployment and their link with crime. His great hope was that he could by his practical "Proposals" and with the support of the Society of Friends, make a real difference to the lives of those of the poor who lived miserably in towns, cities and the countryside. Alas, the support he expected from fellow Quakers was at best, half-hearted. He saw around him many causes for serious concern, much need of reformation, and produced his plans for amelioration which he communicated to the Society of Friends, and where applicable to all magistrates, members of Parliament, all bishops and clergy, even to the heads of every sovereign state in Europe. As his biographer George Clarke wrote:

> "He was one of the most radical thinkers of his day and saw with clarity the vital relationship between crime, poverty, ill-health, unemployment and lack of education; all were symptoms of one massive problem - a grossly maladjusted social and economic system."

In John Bellers' faith human beings were of more importance in the sight of God than were material things; and should be of greater importance to all sincerely religious people, than the search for great position or wealth. He wrote at the beginning of the century when some well known Quaker families did attain both great wealth and position. Were not the Quaker Gurneys known as "Princes among Bankers"? Is this one of the reasons that Bellers' thoughts and schemes were seen as too radical, too disruptive of a social order which was comfortable for many of the more affluent Quakers of his time? John Bellers cared about the poor as fellow children of God; he wrote that they "are like rough diamonds, their worth is unknown". He saw the many social evils of the day and set out "Proposals", practical plans for dealing with mass poverty, unemployment and crime; he proposed free education for all, a free health service with hospitals, general practitioners and research centres nationwide, the abolition of capital punishment, the reform of prisons and the penal law, and of the corrupt methods of electing Members of Parliament. On a larger scale, he proposed a Federation of European states so that difficulties between them could be discussed without recourse to war. He also suggested a Council of all religions. He was indeed a pioneer, many years ahead of his time; over two hundred years have passed by, before many of his plans have been put into effect in our country.

Chief of John Bellers' "Proposals" was for "Colledges of Industry" (the original for Robert Owen's 'Villages of Co-operation'). He was well aware that he needed to appeal to self-interest as well as to a charitable spirit, so he recommended these "Colledges" as ways of reducing the cost of providing for the poor by setting them to work and so to making profit for those who founded them. "Industry", he wrote, "brings plenty":

> "I believe the present idle hands of the poor of this nation are able to raise provision and manufactures that would bring England as much treasure as the mines do Spain."

He costed out all his schemes to demonstrate their pecuniary advantages to all involved. These "Colledges" were to be self-sufficient communities of about 300 persons, young and older, married or single, for education, the training of skills for trades and farming and "mechanical" work. Bellers calculated that 200 would be able to supply the rents and necessities for the whole community and the 100 more would produce enough to make £1000 profit a year for the Founders. In 1723, only two years before he died, John Bellers addressed Parliament on the subject of "Employing the Poor for Profit". Nevertheless there are still no "Colledges of Industry", for our governments still pay out thousands of pounds annually to the "idle poor". He appealed also to Friends, "The Children of Light" to implement his ideas,

> "For the worse they are (i.e. the poor) the more need of endeavouring to mend them; (and why not by this Method, till a better is offered). And it is much more Charity to put the Poor in a way to live by honest Labour, than to maintain them Idle; as it would be to set a man's broken Leg, that he might go himself, rather than always carry him."

Friends in Bristol made an effort in putting these ideas into practice, as did Friends in Clerkenwell - but they set up small institutions which they called "Workhouses" a name much objected to by Bellers as being derogatory. The Clerkenwell "Workhouse" after various

Friends' School, Saffron Walden, Essex.

BY COURTESY OF THE SCHOOL

transformations became eventually the Friends' School in Saffron Walden in Essex. At that school I spent four years of my adolescence; by my time the school was no longer a "Colledge" of John Bellers' dream, but a regular boarding-school, co-educational and liberal in ethos. I think John Bellers would have been grieved to learn that this was the sole result of his "Appeal to the Children of Light": for him, faith and action against every social evil were two sides of the same coin and he would mingle theological views with his practical suggestions, for example in his Essay on the Poor, where he included his own thoughts on God and the Soul; and again in his essay against the "Hanging of Felons" which he ended:

> "With a few Lines of that Religious Guide and Power, by which good actions may be performed."

Of God, he confirmed:

> "God being the most invisible Light, Spirit and Life, he penetrates all Beings and Spirits more thoroughly than the visible Light at Noon-day doth the Air";

> "And therefore the Soul, beyond all other Creatures, is most capable of apprehending the invisible and spiritual Manifestations of God".

23

The Light shows us our actions "whether they be good or evil". In writing of "Divine Worship" he quotes Jesus' words to the woman of Samaria from John 4 vv21-24 (from the R.S.V. 1971):

> "Jesus said to her, 'Woman, believe me, the hour is coming when neither on this mountain nor in Jerusalem will you worship the Father. You worship what you do not know; we worship what we know, for salvation is from the Jews. But the hour is coming, and now is, when the true worshippers will worship the Father in spirit and truth, for such the Father seeks to worship him. God is spirit, and those who worship him must worship in spirit and truth.'"

John Bellers was a faithful attender of Monthly, Quarterly and Yearly Meetings, but his Meeting for Worship was his opportunity to "worship in spirit and truth", for as Jesus said, "God is spirit" and should be so worshipped. George Clarke writes, John Bellers was a "practical mystic", (a "mystic", in the definition which I find acceptable means a person who believes in and finds a direct relationship with the eternal Spirit, which may be called God, the Ultimate Reality, the Numinous or whatever symbolic name is preferred). In "Watch unto Prayer" this is made evident, for it is his testimony to his own deeply held beliefs:

> "Watching is as needful to the soul as breathing is to the body ... As breathing whilst living, is inseparable from the body; so watching is inseparable from the soul, whilst it lives towards God;"...

> "such watchfulness being the true walking in the light, by which all the wiles of the enemy are discovered, and consequently the soul is inspired with immediate Prayer to God for deliverance;"...

> "This is to have conversation in Heaven: a sincere man (upon his watch) though his body stands upon the earth, yet his soul reaches unto heaven."

He goes on to make clear that prayer and watchfulness daily, are the true preparation for a Meeting for Worship, since the mind by "unwatchfulness out of meetings ... is left as the stony, or thorny ground" which makes us "much indisposed for the worship of God" when entering a silent meeting. Bellers ends by referring to several passages of the gospel writers on his theme "Watch and pray, that ye enter not into temptation" (Matt.20v41).

I recall the title of a talk by Howard Collier, to be given to a Young Friends group of which I was a member. "Quakerism", he claimed, "is a tree of mystical roots and practical fruits". John Bellers was a man of "mystical roots and practical fruits", though these fruits were long delayed in reaching maturity because of the lack of support from his contemporaries.

Even so, John Bellers' name follows that of Robert Owen on the "Reformers' Memorial" in Kensal Green Cemetery. I do not know of any Quaker pilgrimage to that spot. Perhaps the Swarthmore Lecture "Beyond the Spirit of the Age" by Jonathan Dale in 1996, on Friends' social testimony and possible action for social reform will inspire Friends to learn more of this great man.

JOHN BELLERS: BOOKS CONSULTED

William C. Braithwaite: *The Second Period of Quakerism*, 2nd edition, William Sessions Ltd, York, 1979.

George Clarke: John Bellers, His Life, Time and Writings, Routledge & Kegan Paul, 1987, and Sessions of York, 1993.

Ed. George Clarke: John Bellers Writings, op cit.

Dictionary of National Biography.

CHAPTER 4

ELIZABETH FRY

JOHN BELLERS died in 1725 and is today very little known and his ideals and practical "Proposals" almost forgotten, even by Quakers; George Clarke's biography went some way towards rectifying this neglect. However, one Quaker reformer is still well known both within and outside the Society of Friends, and that is Elizabeth Fry, who lived from 1780 to 1845. She is considered now as almost a Quaker saint, yet in her own time she was much disapproved of by certain Friends. She was thought to be a neglectful mother in leaving her many children to the care of others while she was engaged in her work of prison reform; she was looked at askance for mingling with people "of the world" and of other Christian denominations and engaging their help in her efforts. The whole family suffered much opprobrium when her husband got into financial difficulties, and this stern disapproval caused her great grief. Nevertheless Elizabeth Fry unlike some of her children, remained a dedicated member of the Society of Friends all her life.

Since Friends were disowned for "marrying out, marrying before a priest" many birthright Friends can claim a marriage connection with other Quaker families. I have some personal interest in Elizabeth Fry as my family, on grandfather Holmes' side have a slight marriage connection with her forebears; we also have a little book lovingly dedicated by Elizabeth Fry to one of my great-great aunts, who was said by my grandmother to have worked with her in some of her prison work.

Elizabeth Fry's biographers, of whom there are many, have given full accounts of her life work as a penal reformer of international renown. I am more interested here in her inner life, the faith which led her to action and empowered her to cope face to face, with evil in criminals, the condemned, women awaiting transportation, the dark underworld of life, as well as with politicians, prison warders and governors of prisons. She moved in high social circles as a member of the Gurney family, and in her later life was invited to share her ideas with Royalty and this she felt as a temptation to pride.

Most of us have seen pictures of her, looking serious in her "plain" Friends dress; as a girl she loved music and dancing, bright colours and fun with her many sisters. She took to the "plain" dress, she said, as a sign of her "convincement" and as a way of pruning the inessential in life so as to live more simply. However, she never lost her appreciation of beauty, of colour in Nature, and in later life wrote of her "acute relish for the beautiful". She was not the solemn person we imagine; her daughter Rachel wrote that she had "a cheerful invigorating influence", a good sense of humour and enjoyment of the comic in life - "I can see her now, with a look of irresistible amusement". Rachel also described how her mother ran her household "with gentle firmness" and "with exceeding love and tenderness to her little children", forbidding severe punishment for their misdemeanours by whipping, for example. She also gave good "care to the domestics, in their mental and bodily needs". She had a particularly melodious voice, speaking sincerely and "melting the listeners with an indescribable quality". Her personality, her inner spiritual life, the dark as well as the illumination, are revealed to some extent in the writings of her daughters and their editing of her diaries.

Elizabeth Fry herself wrote much that was personally revealing in her articles and letters on the care and reformation of prisoners. For example, in her *Observations on the Visiting, Superintending and Government of Female Prisoners* (2nd edition 1827):

> "Much depends on the spirit in which the visitor enters on her work. It must be the spirit, not of judgement, but of mercy. She must not say in her heart, I am more holy than thou; but must rather keep in perpetual remembrance that 'all have sinned, and come short of the glory of God' - that, therefore, great pity is due from us even to the greatest transgressors among our fellow-creatures ... The good principle in the hearts of many abandoned persons may be compared to the sparks of a nearly extinguished fire. By means of the utmost care and attention, united with the most gentle treatment, these may yet be fanned into a flame, but under the operation of a tough and violent hand, they will presently disappear, and may be lost for ever ... For experience shows that if the persons who visit them are harsh in judging and condemning them the effect is hurtful rather than beneficial."

A letter from a niece, quoted by Mrs Pitman (one of her biographers) recalled that:

> "There was no weakness or trouble of mind or body which might not safely be unveiled to her. Whatever various or opposite views, feelings or wishes might be confided to her, all came out again, tinged with her own loving, hopeful spirit. Bitterness of every kind died when entrusted to her."

Mrs Pitman continues that Elizabeth like George Fox "answered that of God" in those she met:

> "She always saw hope for everyone; she invariably found a point of light. The most abandoned must have felt she did not despair for them, either for this world or for another; and this it was that made her irresistible."

So the great question is this; how did she become this "irresistible" person, influencing so many out of darkness into light?

When quite young, in her diary of January 1799 she wrote:

> "The first thing that strikes me is the perception we all have, of being under a power superior to human",

and a month later wrote how doubtfully she responded at first.

> "How dark was my mind for some days! How heavy! I saw duties to be performed that struck me as foolish. I took courage and tried to follow the directions of this voice; I felt enlightened, even happy."

Like the Quietists of the day she believed that God would fill us with his Spirit as and when he wished; the recipient's duty was to be open to receive.

> "The poor creature has only to remain passive."

Aged eighteen, her journal records a spiritual experience shared with the Friends she was visiting at Coalbrookdale.

> "My heart began to feel itself silenced before God ... my mind felt clothed with light as with a raiment."

In general, she lived by spiritual discipline, and told her daughter Rachel towards the end of her life:

> "I can say one thing: since my heart was touched at seventeen years old, I believe I never have awakened from sleep, in sickness or in health, by day or by night, without my first waking thought being how best I might serve the Lord."

She hid periods of depression and lack of faith, writing in 1818:

> "I felt so remarkably low, so unworthy, so unfit, but my scep-
> tical and doubting mind has been convinced of the truth of reli-
> gion, not by the hearing of the ear, but from what I have really
> handled and tasted and known for myself of the work of life,
> may I not say of the power of God unto Salvation."

From her youth her faith was made real by practical action. At home in Earlham before her marriage to Joseph Fry, she had a school for children whom her sisters called "Betsy's Imps". As a young married woman at Plashet she cared for the gypsies and poor Irish in the locality, supplying clothing, medicine, soup in winter as needed, and gave Bibles out to all of them. She was an early convert to the value of vaccination against smallpox and insisted on inoculating as many as she could persuade.

All did not go easily in her life. In 1829 she wrote in her journal:

> "He who seeth in secret, only knows the unutterable depths and
> sorrows I have had to pass through, as well as at other times,
> joys inexpressible and full of glory."

Elizabeth suffered a great deal from her many bereavements through the deaths of friends and family, including some of her children. She, with her husband had to bear the opprobrium of the Society of Friends at the time of her husband's bankruptcy. It is evident that as she grew older she came the more under the influence of Evangelical views among Quakers and the larger society. In Fox's teaching the Inner Light, the Inward Christ was all that was needful to bring us close to God. Elizabeth mentions the Inner Light but rarely, writing more often of the duty to believe in the atoning and saving power of Christ's death on the cross. At the end of her life, when some of her children had left the Society of Friends, she regularly read passages of Scripture with them and wrote on one occasion to them:

> "My dearest children, believing as we do in the Lord as our
> Saviour, one Holy Spirit as our Sanctifier, and one God and
> Father of us all, we can feel united in spirit ..."

When we read of Elizabeth Fry's great work of reform, (built on the proposals of John Bellers, though I do not know if she acknowl-edged this) we feel she was superhuman. Recent biographies, in the modern manner have shown us another side of her life. June Rose in her biography of Elizabeth Fry reveals her many weaknesses. Elizabeth suffered her own Inner Dark: and from her girlhood at times of "low spirits" she was given laudanum, wine, brandy and water. By the early 1840s she took one grain of opium a day (the usual dose being 1/4 of a grain) with a fair amount, perhaps too much, alcohol. She craved these stimulants and claimed she felt ill without them; it seems that she was to some extent, addicted. Elizabeth thanked God for both opium and alcohol as being his gifts, gifts which enabled her to continue to do his work in the world. She would be the first to admit that she was but a frail human being, liable to fall short of her own ideals, unable to be always the person she wished to be.

Elizabeth Fry was accused by fellow Quakers and by others also, of neglecting her husband and even more, of neglecting her children by her preoccupation with her work for penal reform which necessitated long absences from home. Her vision was not as far-sighted as was John Bellers', for unlike him, she did not see the connection between an unjust social and economic system and poverty and crime. Nevertheless many have felt inspired by her great work for prisoners and penal reform, a lasting legacy in this country and others. Elizabeth Fry, herself would discount such praise, being convinced that her work was but the outward result of the inward and invisible grace of God. Any good deed, she believed was inspired by the Holy Spirit and the vision, courage and strength to act came through empowerment by this same Inward Spirit of Christ. She believed with Fox, that it is thus that the "ocean of death and darkness" is "flowed over by the ocean of light and love".

GENERAL BOOKS CONSULTED

Mrs E.R. Pitman: *Elizabeth Fry*, 1884, W.H. Allen & Co., London

June Rose: Elizabeth Fry,1980, Macmillan, London

Janet Whitney: *Elizabeth Fry, Quaker Heroine*, 1938, George Harrap & Co Ltd., London.

PRIMARY SOURCES

"Memoir of the Life of Elizabeth Fry, with Extracts from her Journals and Letters" by two of her daughters, 1847, London, Gilpin.

Susanna Corder: "The Life of Elizabeth Fry, compiled from her Journal as edited by her daughters, and from various other Sources", 1853, W. & F.G. Cash.

CHAPTER 5

NEW ZEALAND

E LIZABETH FRY, born a Gurney and married into another well
known Quaker family is thought of today as being at the heart of
the Quaker "establishment" though some contemporary Quakers took
a different view. Her pioneering work in prison reform is described
in all accounts of 19th-century social history. Elizabeth Fry's first
cousins, the four Wakefield brothers also appear in the history books,
for all were involved in the early colonisation of New Zealand. Their
story, as I relate, differs from the stories of the other Quaker lives I
have described contrasting with their faith and the faithful action which
grew out of that faith. On their maternal side, the Wakefield family
was descended from Robert Barclay, author of the *Apology*; they were
also closely connected by marriage with the tight world of the Quaker
families of the time. The children were, for much of their childhood
in the care of their Quaker grandmother, Priscilla Wakefield, who was
well known as a writer of books for children, and as a practical phil-
anthropist. She was a devoted grandmother, and had a strong influence on the Wakefield boys; nevertheless as adults, none of them were
members of the Society of Friends, though they kept up Quaker
connections. The eldest, Edward Gibbon Wakefield took on some of
his grandmother's philanthropic ideals but was probably more influenced by the political views of his father whose circle of friends included
famous Radicals like Francis Place. As a young man Edward Gibbon
Wakefield stood for Parliament on a Radical manifesto of social reform
but was not elected. He felt that his defeat was due to his lack of ample
funds; he became convinced that he could do good, could ameliorate
the misery of poverty and hardship among the industrial classes by
securing wealth, the only sure way to gain power. Unlike John Bellers
and Elizabeth Fry, whose actions were inspired by deep religious faith
and who relied on "Divine leadings", Edward Gibbon Wakefield relied
on his own vision and his own abilities. He entered diplomatic service,

and became an advisor to Lord Durham, whom he assisted in producing the liberal and far-sighted Durham Report on Canada. He won great praise: for example the entry on Edward Gibbon Wakefield in the Dictionary of National Biography (1899 edition) states "his importance cannot be overestimated" for "all colonial development followed his ideas".

With the backing of Lord Durham and other influential men he started a company for the colonisation of New Zealand, which was later superseded by the New Zealand Company. Gibbon Wakefield was good at public relations and took trouble to gain support from different powerful groups. He was very persuasive and often succeeded in getting city men of probity, Evangelicals, Quakers and speculators alike to go along with his plans and to invest in the New Zealand Land Company. One of the groups he gained support from was the Aborigines' Protection Society, started by the well-known Quaker doctor, Thomas Hodgkin and supported by other Quakers and men who had been prominent in the Anti-Slavery movement such as Fowell Buxton. This Society was informed by Gibbon Wakefield that the arrival of a better class of settler would give the natives an example of civilised behaviour and would forward the aims of helping the Maori and Europeans to live harmoniously together and so build a colony based on Christian values. Had the members of the Aborigines' Protection Society known of one of his despatches to the New Zealand Company, they might have had second thoughts:

> "If the advantage of the Natives were alone to be consulted, it would be better, perhaps that they should remain for ever the savages that they are."

Gibbon Wakefield had a honeyed tongue and was able to speak both enthusiastically and idealistically; he also spoke of the excitement of exploring a newly discovered land. This is how perhaps, he persuaded young John Sylvanus Cotterell (my great-great uncle) and the older and more experienced Frederick Tuckett and Samuel Stephens, all of Quaker families in the Bristol area, to join his company as land surveyors.

Meanwhile the Colonial Office when asked for support was very cautious about getting involved in another territory so far away. Gibbon Wakefield, however, argued before Parliamentary Committees that colonisation could not be halted, and between:

> "Colonisation, desultory, without Law, and fatal to the Natives and a colonisation organised and salutary",

a choice had to be made. Since the Government was slow in making this choice Wakefield went ahead with his own colonising plans in spite of the doubts and disapproval of the Government. There was too, opposition from the Missionary Societies which feared that the coming of large numbers of settlers would cause trouble with the Maori tribes. Even the adulatory article on Edward Gibbon Wakefield in the Dictionary of National Biography (1899) added these words:

> "the great flaw in his character was his lack of scruple in selecting the means for attaining his ends".

His Quaker grandmother Priscilla Wakefield (née Bell) who more or less brought him up from the age of six, wrote in her journal on Edward as a child:

> "My mind painfully engaged in the perverseness of dear little Edward - his obstinacy if he inclines to evil, terrifies me; turned to good it would be a noble firmness."

What prescience!

Gibbon Wakefield's stated aims were to colonise in a "rational manner" and so to deal with two major problems. The first being the chaotic situation in New Zealand where some whalers and some ne'er-do-wells lived lawless and debauched lives: the second problem being the rapidly increasing population in Britain with accompanying poverty, unemployment and growing levels of crime. He was no doubt influenced by the reforming zeal of his father's circle of political Radicals; and his grandmother, Priscilla was a strong Quaker influence throughout her life. Gibbon Wakefield dreamed of building a perfect colony, a Utopia without extremes of wealth or poverty. And last but not least, he wished and needed to make a profit for himself, his Wakefield brothers and the investors in the New Zealand Land Company. As news came through to Britain of the results of colonisation in some distant lands there was unease in many circles, Government, Missionary and Quaker alike. The 1861 edition of *Christian Faith and Practice of the Religious Society of Friends* in reprinting an extract written in 1840 shows their depth of concern:

> "Advices to Emigrants"

> "We would intreat those who may establish themselves in newly settled countries to reflect upon the responsibility which attaches to them when they are the neighbours of uncivilised and heathen tribes. It is an awful and indisputable fact, that most settlements of this description, besides dispossessing the natives of their land without equivalent, have hitherto been

productive of incalculable injury to the moral and physical condition of the native races; which have been thereby more or less reduced in numbers, and in some instances completely exterminated. Earnestly therefore, do we desire that all those who may emigrate to such settlements, may be careful, neither directly nor indirectly to inflict injury on the natives, but on the contrary, in their whole conduct, exhibit the practical character of that religion, which breathes, 'Glory to God in the highest, and on earth peace, goodwill toward men'".

Eventually the British Government moved to annexe New Zealand in 1840, sending their representative William Hobson there to sign a treaty with the Maori chiefs. This Treaty of Waitangi was intended as the basis of a settlement, fair and just to both races. The advice and instruction sent by the Colonial Office to William Hobson in 1839 are similar in spirit to the Quaker "Advice to Emigrants" of a year later. A Law Commissioner, Mr Spain was sent out promptly to investigate and adjudicate on the land sales made by the Maori to the British settlers. It did not take him long to pronounce that the twenty million acres claimed to have been bought by Wakefield's New Zealand Company had not been legally purchased according to Maori tribal custom. This was unfortunate indeed for intending settlers who had bought land in good faith from the Company's agents. The

representatives of the British Government were in the North Island, far from the new settlement of Nelson across the straits in the South Island. There Arthur Wakefield (formerly a captain in the Navy) was busy purchasing land from the Maori in that area. He sent young Sylvanus Cotterell, one of the company's surveyors on exploring expeditions to find more land suitable for farming. Sylvanus reached Tophouse Pass where there is a plaque in his honour, which was unveiled by my sister Phyllis Short as a Cotterell descendant. From there he found a way through the mountains to the valley of the Wairau River which he reported was perfect for the grazing of sheep and for cultivation. Some Maori chiefs, led by the great chief Te Rauparaha, protested in person to Arthur Wakefield that the Wairau plain was not for sale. Nevertheless the survey teams under Tuckett and Cotterell were sent to mark out the land for settlement. Te Rauparaha had been offered and accepted gifts of "tobacco, Wine Sugar and a Blanket". Captain Wakefield expected no further difficulty for he "knew of no situation where either presents or a show of force had not been successful in subduing the local Maoris".

John Sylvanus Cotterell was a Quaker; in fact the first Friends' Meeting for Worship in New Zealand was held in his Nelson house. As a Friend he believed that all human beings were born with the Inward Light and he was ready to "answer that of God" in all whom he met, whether white or brown. So he became friendly with the Maori, started to learn their language and customs and took a young Maori with him on his expeditions as guide and companion. This young man and other Maori warned him that there would be trouble on the Wairau if the survey went ahead, but he was naively prepared to believe in the assurances given to him by Arthur Wakefield that the land had indeed been purchased. Did not the Friends' Yearly Meeting Epistle, though with some warning words, remind all disciples of Christ to:

> "maintain that charity which suffereth long, and is kind: put the best construction upon the conduct and opinions one of another which circumstances will warrant".

In this spirit he put aside any doubts he may have had about the surveying of the Wairau plain. So the survey teams set about their task, cutting pegs from the bush, putting in markers for the plots to be sold to prospective colonists. Maori came to observe and to restate emphatically that the survey should not continue as their chiefs denied having sold this land. The general opinion of the white men was that the New Zealand Company had paid for the land and that the Maori were demanding further payment to be added to what had been agreed, since this problem had occurred elsewhere. This may have been Sylvanus' understanding of the position and in any case he had faith in the word of his employers. The Maori became more insistent that the surveyors should leave and when they did not, the Maori took non-violent action. Every night the markers so painstakingly cut and placed were removed; but even this did not bring the survey to an end. The surveyors built rough huts from local materials into which they placed their tools and other items overnight for safety and continued their work, as best they could.

At last Te Rauparaha and his kinsman chief Te Rangiheata arrived for a "korero" or formal talk. They were accompanied by about eighty men, some of whom were armed with guns but who cannot have intended upon armed conflict as some had their women and children with them. Again the Maori chiefs asked the surveyors to leave the area, and not to return until the Law Commissioner had made his adjudication in a few days' time; this adjudication the Maori said that they would accept and abide by. These demands were met with total and angry rejection by the Europeans, the "pakeha"; at this the chiefs ordered their men to take out from the makeshift huts everything belonging to the "pakeha", and then to burn the huts which, as they pointed out, were built of local timber and reeds. Thereupon Sylvanus Cotterell was sent with an urgent message to Nelson, where Arthur Wakefield and the local magistrate, Thompson ordered the arrest of both chiefs for arson, and an armed party was sent to put this order into effect. Cotterell and Tuckett, the two Quakers surveyors were appalled at this trumped-up charge. However, they returned with this party in the hope that they could influence events in a peaceful direction. This was not to be: for while attempts were made to handcuff and arrest the two chiefs, someone fired a shot and immediately there was gunfire from both sides. A few fled, Fred Tuckett among them; others were killed including six Maori. Te Rangiheata saw his wife killed and this act so enraged him that there was a terrible consequence for those who surrendered, among them Sylvanus. They were killed by the axe or knife as "utu", the revenge permitted by Maori custom. In total twenty-two Europeans were killed and their names are on the commemorative monument which still stands by the Wairau. Reports of what actually happened are confused and there are differing accounts of Sylvanus' death. He carried no weapon and was known as a friend to the Maori and a reconciler, but this had not saved his life.

Following this affair, Mr Spain the Law Commissioner and Fitzroy the then governor set up an Enquiry. They found in favour of the

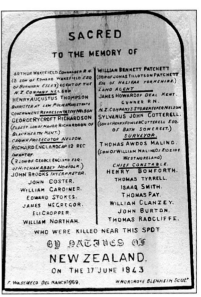

Maori, whose claim to have the right in the matter was upheld. Fitzroy therefore, condemned the killings but refused to punish the Maori, to the fury of the white settlers, who referred to the affair as the "Wairau Massacre". Modern historians write of the "Wairau Incident" and are agreed that the memory of this event played a part in embittering and inflaming racial antagonism on both sides.

What does this grievous tale have to tell us? The evidence I have read is somewhat ambiguous: some historians incline towards acceptance of the Wakefield brothers' assertions that they were fighting the evils of the anarchic state of colonisation in New Zealand, at the same time easing, through emigration, the social problems of Britain; in their view, bringing light to the darkness on both sides of the world. Other historians, particularly Maori scholars of the present day, consider them as hypocrites, feathering their own nests with little regard for the lives and rights of the native people. Many in the home country, many Quakers such as Thomas Hodgkin, the Cotterell, Tuckett and Stephens families, and Edward Gibbon' first wife's family thought well of the Wakefield brothers, and of Edward Gibbon in particular. Was he not held in high esteem by Lord Durham? Was he not brought up by the famous Priscilla Wakefield? And was he not of honourable Quaker lineage and cousin to the Frys and Gurneys? How could such a person be a deceiver of the Maori and unscrupulous in his dealings? Matt. Chap.10 v.16 advises all followers of Jesus to be "wise as serpents and harmless as doves". These Quaker supporters of Edward Gibbon Wakefield were harmless, no doubt, but lacking, it seems in wisdom and the gift of discernment. Were they simply being Quakerly in expecting to find "that of God", (which was no doubt present) in Gibbon Wakefield and unable because unwilling, to perceive that he might be a wolf in sheep's clothing? It is plain that some of his actions caused others to suffer by the wrongdoing of his New Zealand Company.

Perhaps these Friends should have been alerted by the past history of two of the Wakefield brothers, who had both served prison sentences. In 1816, pursuing his desire for wealth, Gibbon Wakefield had eloped with an heiress and married her; sadly, she died later in childbirth. Ten years later, he persuaded his brother William to assist him in eloping with another heiress, this time an under-age schoolgirl, whom he carried off to Gretna Green. Her relatives acted swiftly, preventing the couple from crossing the Channel to France. This marriage was annulled by Act of Parliament: Edward was sent to Newgate, and William as his accomplice, to Lancaster Gaol. (In 1828 Edward was visited in Newgate by Elizabeth Fry, but I have found no details of this meeting.)

Friends, as do all Christians, believe in the possibility of repentance, forgiveness and reformation of life. These past events it seems, were not held against him, and Gibbon Wakefield was looked upon in many quarters as an honourable man. Nevertheless there were those who did not agree with this estimation. Keith Sinclair, the historian of New Zealand writes of him as a:

> "sort of intellectual confidence man, adroit, resilient, yet regarded with unalterable suspicion by those out of the range of his persuasive voice and the fascination of his personality."

I have read some of the papers and letters home of John Sylvanus Cotterell which are preserved in the Alexander Turnbull Library in Wellington, New Zealand and in the Friends' Meeting House in Nelson in the South Island, where Cotterell had made his home. These show him to have been a likeable young man full of a youthful sense of adventure, coupled with idealism and a social conscience; he was killed when only twenty-three. In the volume of biographical sketches by Audrey and James Brodie entitled *Seeking a New land: Quakers in New Zealand* we learn that John Sylvanus "became interested in colonisation and the welfare of the aborigines". When he was appointed to go to New Zealand he did so, partly to work as a surveyor, but also "to further his interest in the welfare of the Maori inhabitants". It was taken for granted by Evangelicals, including Quakers of the time, that it was a right and a duty to take the Christian religion to the heathen in far-off lands. He had this serious side, but was also full of joie-de-vivre, appreciating the land and native peoples, observing the flora and fauna with delight, and excited by his explorations. He was young and naïve and his trust proved to be tragically misplaced. Did any good come from the tragic deaths of Maori and "pakeha" by the Wairau river? I can see only evil and the increase of hatred and suspicion in years to come.

Now to the unexpected ending of this story, an intriguing connection with the present generation. My sister and brother-in-law, Phyl and Joe Short returned from India in 1953 to live in New Zealand, Joe's native country, with their four children. Their son Murray Rodwell Short chose to engage in social work in an area of largely Maori population in the same spirit which prompted his forebear John Sylvanus Cotterell more than one hundred and fifty years ago. Thus he met and married Niwa Kereama, a member of the Tuhoe tribe, descended on her father's side from Te Rauparaha. The marriage of Murray and Niwa has brought great gifts of experiences and understanding to Phyllis and her family. When Joe Short died they held a "wake" similar to a Maori "tangi" which was attended by the Maori relations as well as by other family members. Recently, Phyllis, her sons and daughters and grand-children were part of the "tangi" for Niwa's father after he died. This took place on his home "marae" the communal gathering-place. I am happy to report that though small in numbers, Friends of New Zealand Yearly Meeting are working with those who aim at obtaining full equality and justice in all respects for Maori and "Pakeha" alike. In a recent letter Phyl Short writes that:

> "the Government and Tribal authorities are attempting, in this generation to settle longstanding historic grievances".

NEW ZEALAND: J.S.COTTERELL

BOOKS CONSULTED

Paul Bloomfield: *Edward Gibbon Wakefield in the series Builders of the British Commonwealth*, Longmans, London, 1961.

Audrey & James Brodie: *Seeking a New Land: Quakers in New Zealand. A volume of biographical sketches*, Quaker Historical MS published for New Zealand Yearly Meeting of the Society of Friends by Beech Tree Press, Wellington, NZ, 1993.

Patricia Burns: *Te Rauparaha*, Ch.34, A.H.& W. Reed, Auckland, New Zealand, 1996.

Dictionary of National Biography, 1899 & 1909 editions.

Journal of the Friends' Historical Society, vol.20, 1923.

Elsie Locke: *Journal Under Warning*, Oxford University Press, Auckland & London, 1983.

Ed. G.W. Rice: *Oxford History of New Zealand*, 2nd edition, Oxford University Press, Oxford, 1992.

Theodore Rigg: *Surveyor, Explorer, Idealist*; report in Nelson Evening Mail, August 15, 1957, of his address to the Nelson Historical Society.

Theodore Rigg: *History of the Society of Friends in Nelson and Nelson Explorer and Surveyor: John Sylvanus Cotterell 1819-1843*, MS in the Nelson Provincial Museum, New Zealand.

Keith Sinclair: *History of New Zealand*, Pelican original, Penguin Books, Allen Lane, London, Reprinted 1969.

Symposium organised by the Alexander Turnbull Library, National Library, Wellington, New Zealand, *A Reassessment of Edward Gibbon Wakefield*. Papers published by the Library, 1997.

SOURCE MATERIAL

John Sylvanus Cotterell: letters and reports in the Dr. F.A. Bett Collection, Nelson Provincial Museum, South Island, New Zealand.

J.S.C.'s letters and papers in the care of The Friends Meeting, Nelson, South Island, New Zealand.

J.S.C.'s letters in the Alexander Turnbull Library, The National Library of New Zealand, Wellington, New Zealand.

The Friend, 1st mo. 1944, 5th mo. 1845 Reports of John Sylvanus Cotterell's death and copies of letters to his relatives in Bath.

Letters of John Sylvanus Cotterell to his mother in Bath (courtesy of Patricia Frood (née Cotterell). Priscilla Wakefield in *The Friend* 6, 1848.

Samuel Stephens (Principal surveyor of the New Zealand Company) Reports on surveys and the death of John Sylvanus Cotterell, The Nelson Provincial Museum, New Zealand.

CHAPTER 6

EVANGELICALISM: MY PARENTS

IN READING Elizabeth Fry's journals and her account of her own
spiritual journey, it is evident that from the time she became a
"plain Friend" an Evangelical form of Quakerism became her faith.
She was but one of many Friends to follow this path, for as the years
of the nineteenth century went by, the Society of Friends as a whole
moved towards Evangelicalism. John Sylvanus Cotterell's faith was of
this kind, as was later, in the early days of the new century, the
Quakerism of my parents, particularly of my father. Evangelical
Quakerism had a message to give somewhat different from the message
proclaimed by George Fox and seventeenth-century Friends. Robert
Barclay in his Apology wrote that the Inward Christ, the Inner Light
was the "primary rule" and the Scriptures the "secondary rule".
Evangelical Friends tended to reverse this order, considering the Bible
to be the chief authority for faith. Some London Yearly Meeting
Epistles (for example of 1833) went so far as to state that the "leadings" of the Inner Light were "delusions". The sinfulness of humanity
was emphasised; the only way to pass from the darkness of sin was for
each individual to come to the Cross and to accept Christ's sacrifice
as "atonement" for all sins and so to be "saved", with the promise of
Heaven in the next life. Otherwise, since sinfulness was our basic
human condition, without this "salvation", after death would come
Hell. As Roger Wilson has written in his *Manchester, Manchester and
Manchester Again* (1990 Friends' Historical Society):

> "sin, blood, punishment, atonement, salvation are always on the
> lips of evangelical Friends".

So our failures, our shortcomings, our wrongdoing, our inner dark
were to be transmuted, not by "walking in he Light", as Fox taught,
but by the acceptance of Christ's vicarious sacrifice on the cross. The
saving of the individual was seen as imperative, for unlike John Bellers'

41

view that the economic and social system needed to be changed and thus help to change the individual, most Evangelicals believed that poverty, unemployment, crime were the results of individual failure to "live in the Light". Nevertheless, where individuals were not considered responsible for their condition or their suffering, Friends were ready with practical action; they actively supported the anti-slavery movement for example, and were very much engaged in relieving the starving in Ireland at the time of the Great Hunger. Here Friends saw "death and darkness", and brought what "light and love" they could at both a spiritual and practical level.

Roger Wilson gives a vivid description of the struggle at the level of Preparatory, Monthly. Quarterly and Yearly Meeting which took place between the older and original form of Quakerism and the new Evangelical influence. Manchester, in both Hardshaw East and West Monthly Meetings contained a great enough number of "weighty" Friends of the Evangelical persuasion, to stand against the growth of more liberal beliefs and modern attitudes to the Bible. Even the holding of the 1895 Manchester Conference, which allowed a fresh wind to blow through the Society, did not affect the beliefs of some of these Evangelical Friends. They supported the Friends Foreign Mission Association for the conversion of the heathen in faraway countries; they also supported the Friends Home Mission Committee, which was working at a national level to convert the unconverted English from their state of darkness to the Light of the Gospel. Manchester Friends, as did Meetings in cities such as Darlington and Birmingham, set up a city Mission, First Day Schools and Adult Schools. There was a wave of great enthusiasm for the "saving of souls from damnation" by "bringing them to the foot of the Cross". My father, John Rodwell, at the age of nineteen joined the Society of Friends in Manchester and was caught up in this enthusiasm, soon becoming active in the Friends' Mission work. He used to tell of Mission meetings he attended and sometimes led, where the hall was filled with down and outs, drunks and despairing men. There would be a short talk followed by prayer and hymns such as those of Moody and Sankey. A favourite was

"Throw out the life-line, somebody's sinking today-ay-ay!"

The life-line was Jesus Christ and the belief that His saving work on the cross, when accepted would bring forgiveness, redemption and the possibility of turning from evil in this life and the hope of heaven in the next. Those who were thus saved would in future live sober, hard-working and prudent lives, which would bring not only inner joy and peace, but material rewards also. Such a saved soul would be a better husband, father and workman, able to improve himself and therefore the situation of himself and that of his family.

My father, having heard the call to mission work, decided that he needed to share in the rough life of some who attended the Friends' Mission, so as to understand better their hardships and temptations. He set off on the road to Derby (about sixty miles distant) dressed as a tramp or an unemployed man searching for work. An account of his journey was written by my brother Henry and published in his *China Mission*. The experience was quite a shock to my father, but of course he knew he would return to a comfortable home, clean clothes, good food and a welcome. He did gain sympathy and more understanding of the lives of some unfortunates.

After this apprenticeship in Mission work in Manchester, John Rodwell became a travelling missionary for the Friends' Home Mission Committee. He travelled in a horse drawn van mostly in rural areas, preaching to the local people. I have a photograph of him as he cooked a meal on a camp-fire at a road-side, the vehicle parked behind him

John Porter Rodwell, c1906.

43

with the words painted on its side in large letters "Friends Home Mission. The Wages of Sin are Death; the Gift of God is Eternal Life". This must have been in the early years of the century, for by 1906 John Rodwell had been accepted by the Friends Foreign Mission Association for training as a Quaker missionary in China. In Manchester he had been apprenticed to a pharmacist with a view to becoming a dispensing chemist; this background was of use when he entered Livingstone College in London for medical training and practical experience. He said years later, that when recalling those days he felt it had been wrong for him and his fellow students to be allowed to try their hands in dental and other treatment in some hospital for the poor in the locality. Nevertheless this training, particularly in tropical illnesses was invaluable to him when in China.

On his first "furlough" my father met my mother at Woodbrooke College, and they soon after, became engaged. Dorothy Holmes had been brought up in very different circumstances from my father in his working class family. My grandfather's family, the Holmes' like my grandmother's family, the Cotterells had been Quakers for generations and always fairly affluent. Arthur Stansfield Holmes was a tea and coffee merchant, well established in the city of Chester and able to provide a comfortable home for his wife and four children. They lived in a commodious house where there were two servants and a nanny, later to be replaced by a governess for the children as they grew older. The religious atmosphere was strong and somewhat evangelical for Arthur Holmes had been brought up in the Evangelical tradition, reinforced at the Quaker school he was sent to, the Stramongate School in Kendal. A letter from school to his father (in the possession of our family today) demonstrates that fear and a sense of guilt were to be the method of discipline for the creating of goodness, in contrast to Fox's emphasis on love and light as the conquerors of darkness. Here is the little boy's letter to his father, Alexander Holmes:-

"My dear pappa

Daniel was cast in the den of lions. and we are often cast in the den of saten but the Lord will (help?) if we pray to him. We must follow him in A narrow path and we must not step out of it. Samuel was a judge and we must be a judge over saten or else we will not go to Heaven but to a place of misery and will be fastened with chains and where fier and brimstone will be burning and we will be burning for ever and ever. it is awful, no human being can describe it. but Heaven is splendid and the lord is so shining and he lights all Heaven and all is peace and happyness. no trouble and tears for Jesus wipes them all away and where the wicked seace from trublering and the weary are at rest let us be faithful and good to love God and keep his commandments and too be kind and to put away evel and crows words and then what will happen, then we will go to Heaven but not if we swar and are not kind then we will go to hell and murder and do not keep the commandments. so let us be good and go to Heaven and dear Lucy is there and when we die Lucy will come to meet us and she will lead us to God, and at the last day Lucy and all people will arise that have died, and God will judge them all and us as well and some hundred of hundreds will go to heaven and hundreds of hundreds will go to hell and do let us be sum to go to Heaven and not to hell so we will have to be good if we want to go to Heaven and then we will sing with God and the angles like this peace around the throne of God in Heaven ten thousand children stand children whose sins are all forgiven a holy happy band.

From your son Arthur Holmes."

John Porter Rodwell,
1885-1949.

Dorothy Rodwell (née Holmes),
1888-1951.

Arthur Holmes continued the evangelical tradition in his home; Dorothy, with the other members of the household attended daily Bible readings by her father and was expected to learn passages from the Bible by heart. The whole family went faithfully to the Friends' Meeting in Chester, where Dorothy as a young adult was one of the teachers of the Sunday School run by the Meeting for local poor children. Thankfully we would never today see a photograph of such children, with unkempt hair, over-large hand-me-down jackets with frayed edges at the wrists, boots with toes peeping out of holes, some with unchildlike expressions on their faces.

Dorothy and her sisters and brother were well-dressed and well-shod and cared for at home. After some years being taught by a governess, Dorothy went first to the Queen Margaret School in Chester, then as a boarder to the Friends' school, "The Mount" in York. She decided early that she wished to train as a teacher and unusually for that time continued with higher education by going to Westfield College, University of London. This was a college for "evangelical females" set up to "counteract the atheism of Oxford and Cambridge"; Westfield had a reputation for turning out head-mistresses and missionaries, which may have influenced Arthur Holmes to consider such an education suitable for his daughter.

In 1914 Dorothy, as had John earlier, "heard the call" to the mission field and offered for service with the Friends Foreign Mission Association. In their record of her background she is noted as having been active in Sunday School and Women's Adult School work in Chester and had been a keen member of the Christian Union at Westfield. The FFMA sent her to study at Woodbrooke (where she met her future husband, John Rodwell) then for a course of Sunday School teaching at Westhill College. Dorothy and John's engagement was marred by the disapproval of Dorothy's mother, Lucy Beatrice Holmes (née Cotterell). Sadly some Friends around the turn of the century, and perhaps earlier, were both Quaker and social snobs. John's parents had joined the Society of Friends through being members of an Adult School, and such were not always welcomed by birth-right Friends, who thought of themselves as the "real" Friends! Lucy wrote to her daughter that she should not marry John Porter Rodwell "as he was not a gentleman". My mother replied in defence that "as a missionary, he was a Christian and a gentleman". They were married in Chester Friends' Meeting House and shortly after, sailed for China, reaching Chungking in December 1915.

EVANGELICALISM

BOOKS CONSULTED

Mollie Grubb (now Hooper): *The Beaconite Separation*, Journal of the Friends Historical Society, Vol. 55, no. 6.

Alistair Heron,: *Quakers in Britain, a century of change*, Curlew Graphics, 1995.

Rufus Jones: *The Later Periods of Quakerism*, Vol. 2, Macmillan & Co. Ltd., London, 1921.

John Punshon: *Portrait in Grey*, Quaker Home Service, London, 1984.

Roger Wilson: Manchester, *Manchester and Manchester Again.* Friends' Historical Society Occasional Series, No. 1, 1990.

PRIMARY SOURCES

Family letters and papers.

Friends Foreign Mission Association records (Friends House Library).

CHAPTER 7

CHINA MISSION

JOHN AND DOROTHY RODWELL were following in the footsteps of earlier Quaker missionaries in China, sent out from the turn of the century. All felt they were obeying the New Testament injunction to preach the gospel throughout the world, bringing the light of Christ into the darkness of heathen hearts; this was the sole basis for the founding of the Friends Foreign Mission Association in 1868. From the 1850's, the Society of Friends, with other denominations, were much concerned by the exporting of opium from India to China. This trade was lucrative for the British, but injurious to the Chinese and totally against the wishes of the Chinese authorities. During and after the Opium Wars many were deeply ashamed of British involvement in this trade, and Quakers with other members of the "Anglo-Oriental Society for the Suppression of the Opium Trade" opposed it by all possible means. This concern for the Chinese people on whom opium was being forced, was one of the reasons for the Friends Foreign Mission Association becoming involved in China. There was the hope that some amends could be made for this wrong done to China; there was also the hope that even the evils of opium addiction could be lessened by the acceptance of Christ as Saviour, by Chinese people.

In 1908 the FFMA Report appealed for "more missionaries and distinctly evangelistic ones", "willing to testify to the Saviour", not only for "preaching and oversight but for training the native helpers". With the benefit of hindsight it is evident that the FFMA understanding of the situation in China and of the position of the missionaries there was somewhat simplistic. Easy enough to think of bringing light into dark places, not so easy to appreciate and accept that foreigners in China were forced to live and work in grey areas of compromise. This was particularly true for the missionaries, who were

Dorothy Rodwell, accompanied by military escort on the bank of the River Yangtse.

BY COURTESY OF THE RODWELL FAMILY

given a privileged position by the unequal Treaties which strong Western nations had forced upon the Chinese. "Extra-territoriality" meant that foreigners, and in some cases, Chinese converts to the Christian faith, who broke any law were not tried by Chinese courts but by European law. Missionaries and mission properties were protected by these Treaties and ultimately, by the military forces of Western nations. Local Chinese magistrates were held accountable for any violence done to Europeans, especially to missionaries, and as I myself remember, when on journeys in troublous times we were provided with a Chinese military escort. If Friends were unable to accept this situation, it would mean that they could not work in China at all.

In 1908 after his period of training my father was accepted by the FFMA, specifically to be an evangelist. His religious beliefs at that time coincided with those of the FFMA, that the first duty of every Christian was to spread the knowledge of the Gospel as revealed in the New Testament. There were unique Quaker elements such as their belief in the Inward Light which made it possible for every human being to respond to this message, this response being their spiritual baptism. No outward sacraments such as "water baptism" and the taking of Communion were necessary for salvation. The meetings conducted by the Quaker missionaries were in the style of the Evening Meetings with which they were accustomed at home: preaching, reading and expounding the Gospels with some hymns and vocal prayers. The serious enquirers and attenders, the more mature, were encouraged to attend the silent Meetings for Worship and to become "Probationers" before applying for their membership of the Society of Friends, steps which some took. My mother, Dorothy Holmes was accepted as a teacher by the FFMA before her marriage to my father in 1915. She had not such strong evangelical beliefs as some other Quaker missionaries but would still feel her first duty was to tell the Chinese of the one true God, as revealed in the life and teaching of Jesus. She wrote in an early letter to Friends:

> "At home one often hears of the educated Chinese Confucianist, with his ancient classics and high ethical standard, who worships no images. Once out here probably your ideas like mine would need to be modified. For the popular religion is not Confucianism - that only belongs to the literary few - the mass of the people are idol worshippers, who live in terror of evil spirits, in sickness or calamity they spend their little all in hiring priests to propitiate demons, or in visiting shrines".

I recall as a child walking with a couple who had a fine healthy boy, and my puzzlement at their references to him as a poor creature, not worthy of the jealous attention of evil spirits. Outside our house in Chengtu my brother and I would sometimes see a procession of people following an idol, carried aloft, and offering its priests money for prayers to protect them from danger or disease. In the hill-country we would wander in to temples where the priests, for a sum, permitted the supplicant who for example, suffered with abdominal pain, to rub the stomach of an idol or statue of the Buddha. Once we went into a temple where in addition to the smiling figure of the Buddha, there were enormous and terrifying statues and wall-paintings of angry and ferocious dark-skinned gods. As was usual a priest when paid, would light some incense and pray for your safety, your health, and your protection from evil forces. We today can hardly imagine living in a world where the propitiation of gods and demons is essential to life itself. As John Macmurray once wrote, "freedom from fear is the greatest gift of the faith which Jesus taught"; this faith in a loving and caring Creator was to be shared with the Chinese, who would thus be freed to love this one true God. The second great commandment, to love our neighbours as ourselves, led all the Christian missionaries of whatever denomination to try to bring practical help in combating the terrible diseases suffered by all social classes of the population.

Tuberculosis, smallpox, leprosy, malaria, parasitic infestation, dysentery and cholera were common causes of sickness and often, early death. Infant and maternal mortality were high throughout the country. Missionaries set up vaccination centres against smallpox; dispensaries and hospitals were built, at first for men only but later for women too, as the Chinese began to trust the Western doctors. My father helped in the dispensaries of the Quaker missions, and as he told us later, when there was no doctor available but the patients kept coming, he treated them as best he could. At least he had medical books, some knowledge, and drugs for use in some diseases such as quinine for malaria. He could and did help to clean up the wounds of battle casualties, he removed bullets and amputated limbs where this was a matter of life or death. His basic medical training stood him in good stead in all his years in China. In the FFMA reports we learn that my mother too, sometimes helped with midwifery cases.

In addition to their medical work, all the missionaries tried to educate people in the importance of cleanliness, pure water and hygienically prepared food. In spite of their own knowledge and precautions, my parents lost their four year old daughter Helen, from dysentery and almost lost my brother through the same disease. Today it is accepted that many Chinese traditional herbal preparations and

Family visit to Helen's grave in Tungchwan, 1922.
BY COURTESY OF THE
RODWELL FAMILY

51

for example, acupuncture, are successful in treating many ills of the body. Nevertheless, in the early years of this century there was general ignorance of the causes of disease, and to the Western scientific view, some quite extraordinary suggestions for cures were accepted. In time of plague, for example, the wearing of amulets and the carrying of certain animal bones on the person were recommended by the authorities as efficacious methods of prevention.

The Quakers in West China, with similar motives as the founders of the First Day Schools and Adult Schools in Britain, set up primary and secondary schools and later joined with other denominational missionary bodies in the creation of the West China Union University of Chengtu - which still exists today, though in a slightly different form.

In the schools and this university, they expected to transform ignorance into real understanding of modern ideas such as in science and medicine, and to provide knowledge of the world beyond China. Women were gradually given the opportunity of education in Quaker and other schools and later, even of entering the West China Union University. This was an amazing change for women and in the attitudes of men towards women in China. For centuries women had led lives of Confucian obedience to their fathers and husbands, always subordinate to men who often treated them as being of little account. In the family, males alone could perform the essential ceremonies for dead ancestors, something of central importance in Chinese culture. For this and other reasons female infanticide was a frequent occurrence; for example, I have seen what looked like bundles of ragged cloth floating in the water on our way downriver in 1926, which were actually, abandoned girl babies. My mother was sometimes told by a Chinese woman of girl babies she had not "picked up" at the time of birth. According to recent reports in the media, to a lesser extent this attitude persists in the twenty first century. The age-old custom of foot-binding, another example of the oppression suffered by most women of all classes (except the Manchus and the peasants who had to labour in the fields) was still general in the 1920s. I remember hearing the gardener's little daughter weeping bitterly, no longer playing about outside, and being told she was suffering the breaking of bones for foot-binding. Dear Mrs Wang, who cared for us children while mother was teaching, had bound feet and hobbled about as best she could in a curious waddling gait which was accepted as normal.

Quakers and all missionaries tried to raise the status of women by the teaching of Jesus that all human beings, regardless of gender, age

*J.P.R. Journey on the
River Yangtse.*
BY COURTESY OF THE
RODWELL FAMILY

or colour were equally children of God, all were loved by their Creator
and should be given love and respect by us. Chinese marriage were
arranged through family connections and was considered a binding
contract.   Back in England, years later my parents sometimes
commented how well such arranged marriages often worked, bringing
happiness and stability to the couple concerned. Marriage in China
did not mean that the men were faithful husbands or monogamous.
There were always "tea-garden girls" and those who were wealthy
enough to support a large household took one or more concubines;
some men also expected sexual favours from the girls sold into rich
families by their poverty-stricken parents. Wives and concubines,
especially when superseded, sometimes attempted suicide.   The
American Quaker, Margaret Simkin, reported in her *Letters from
Szechwan* (1924) that there have "been known to have been three
brides here in the hospital at the same time, all attempted suicides".
The reports sent back to the FFMA mentioned that being called out
for cases of suicide, usually of girls and women occurred from time to
time. My mother told me that once she had an urgent call to a household where a concubine was very ill, through having an obstruction
in her stomach. The doctor and my father were both away, but as the
situation seemed desperate my mother set off with a medical book and
a stomach pump. It turned out that concubine number one had been
put to one side for concubine number two; in her distress and jealousy she had swallowed a jade necklace. My mother's efforts were

53

eventually successful but the young woman received scant sympathy, rather she was blamed for trying to do away with herself by using such valuable jewellery. Life was held cheap, especially the lives of women and girls. This general lack of respect and concern for women, for any poor, sick and suffering human being came as a great shock to Europeans then, and also many years later, to the men and women of the Friends Ambulance Unit during the Second World War, as Bernard Llewellyn recalled in his autobiography.

Mission House at Chin Lung Kai, Chengtu.
BY COURTESY OF FRIENDS HOUSE LIBRARY

54

CHAPTER 8

CHINA FROM 1908

CHINA, when my father arrived in 1908 was in a state of ferment which eventually resulted in the overthrow of the ruling Manchus. Following this Revolution in 1911, Szechwan province entered a period of confusion and lawlessness. Banditry was widespread, and the area between Chungking and Suining was seriously affected with villages attacked, trade hampered and travelling dangerous for the Chinese though less so for us foreigners, who were protected by Treaties and by the naval gunboats on the Yangste river. There was a civil war going on with a Northern army in Szechwan fighting the army of Southerners. From about the time of my mother's arrival in 1915, Szechwan was "divided between warring and predatory generals. The 'warlord era' had begun" and continued for more than two decades.

Dorothy and John wrote many personal letters to their parents and more formal ones for interested members of the Society of Friends and Reports for the FFMA. These give a vivid picture of some of the dangers which the missionary in West China faced from time to time in that period. There was one occasion when my parents were separated at the time of my brother Henry's birth in January 1918, my father being held up by fighting in the Tungliang area while my mother was staying with the Wighams in Suining. My mother wrote to Friends on January 31st:

"Before long we were in the midst of a rattle of rifle fire which continued incessantly all day. The Hospital and the house were in the line of fire; bullets constantly hit the roofs, a number struck the house, some coming in through the windows. My room was on the sheltered side of the house but one bullet came in through the window of another room", and was found nestling in the drawer among my new-born brother Henry's baby clothes. Little Helen, then two years old, could not understand why she was not allowed to play outside! My mother continued with this understatement:

"It wasn't a pleasant experience to lie there and listen to the whizz of passing bullets and the clatter as they hit the house or tiles and you can well imagine how thankful we were when, at dusk, the Southerners took the city, the bugles sounded to cease firing".

Meanwhile John Rodwell was in the city of Tungliang which had been occupied by one army which then left, sending back some soldiers to collect the sum of 30,000 taels from the inhabitants. They, having paid 10,000 of the 30,000 taels demanded, decided enough was enough, and sent messengers to acquaint the other army of their changed allegiance. My father writes:

"The result was that different bodies of soldiers under different commanders and acting independently of each other at once began to march to Tungliang"

declaring that they were saving the city and giving the citizens protection. More and more troops:

"arrived until the city seemed full of them, every temple, the inns and every public place were crowded with them. There seemed a great lack of discipline, soldiers crowded the streets, brow-beating the people, buying goods only tendering a few cash in payment ... all shops were closed, the people refused to do business and refugees began to come to our church premises".

Eventually fighting broke out between two of these groups of soldiers on Christmas morning 1918.

"Immediately a terrible panic seized the city and people fled hither and thither seeking shelter. Three families below (i.e. the mission walls) I saw crouching behind the buildings in mortal terror of their lives. Even after I had persuaded them to come up here for refuge they refused to leave the shelter of the compound walls."

At long last things calmed down and my father was able to rejoin his wife and to see his baby son in Suining.

In spite of the sporadic fighting in the early twenties there were periods of peaceful life when Dorothy and John were able to get to know many different Chinese people and to make some true and lasting friendships. They are said by friends and colleagues to have had a real gift of getting to know people on a friendly and yet deep level. At that time some may have thought of the Chinese in a somewhat stereotypical way as, for example, devious, inscrutable and without humour. Far from the truth! My father had an impish sense of humour and told many a joke which brought a warm response from his Chinese hearers. On some occasions this ability got him out of a tight corner. My parents admired the fortitude, resilience and hopefulness of many of the Chinese in some very difficult circumstances; and they appreciated the high regard that the deeper, more scholarly thinkers held for the teachings of Lao Tse, the Buddha and Confucius. In many respects these teachings are remarkably like the teachings of Jesus, who lived so many years later. It was evident that the Chinese were not living up to these high moral principles, but after the First World War, missionaries could make no claim that the Christian nations acted as Christians, either.

My parents were devoted to one another, and were sustained in the many difficult times of their lives by their love and their faith. I can remember quite vividly a particularly dangerous time that our family lived through. In February 1924 during a lull in the civil war which plagued Szechwan a group of Friends, British and Chinese, left Tungchwan for the Friends "Yearly Meeting" which was to be held in Chengtu, the capital. Our family, consisting of parents and three children and our much-loved Mrs Wang, had just arrived in Tungchwan in time to be involved in renewed warfare between the Northern and Southern armies. My father wrote to Friends in London:

> "Our house was in the line of fire so we barricaded the study downstairs with boxes and baggage (as yet unpacked) and put the children to bed on the floor."

The Northerners took the city and some men of the defeated troops "with the perspiration streaming down their faces and with the fear of death on them" begged for,

> "admittance into the Mission compound ... whilst we were negotiating there were sounds of the approach of the enemy ... It was a most difficult situation, to let them in would mean that the 'conquering heroes' might force their way into the

compound in search of them, and then all have suffered, and yet we could hardly see them shot at our very gates".

They were sent round to the Girls' Day School (fortunately empty at that time) and were peacefully disarmed by the victors in the morning. Throughout the following days the city was looted, and the hospital as well. The store room was broken open and blankets and other items taken away.

"Dr Lucy Harris has been simply splendid throughout, most bravely tackling all sorts of difficult situations as well as superintending the dressing of about 300 wounded ... Two days ago we received word that a number of small boats had arrived with over 100 wounded and we were requested to change their dressings. ,,, a Hospital nurse, a servant, a young school teacher and I took on the job ... their wounds had not been dressed for three days and some were in a horrible septic condition."

A short time after these events it must have been a relief to my parents to be informed that they "were appointed to reside in Chengtu with over sight of the schools and meeting".

Afternoon tea under the arbour in the Mission House, Chengtu (1925?).
(unknown guest), Joan(na), JPR, (unknown guest), DHR, Phyllis, Rose Tebbutt,
her father, Henry.

CHAPTER 9

CHANGE AND GROWTH

DURING 1914/15 my father had been on furlough in England; there he attended courses on the New Testament and on Quakerism at Woodbrooke, (a College in Birmingham for Quaker studies) where he met my mother who was already training as a missionary teacher with the FFMA. They both studied the New Testament with the renowned scholar Rendel Harris, and these and other studies helped to change and develop their Christian faith. Then came the First World War, and John Rodwell joined the Friends War Victims' relief work in France. He did what he felt was a reasonable stint in rebuilding shattered homes - for it was generally agreed that the war would be over in a few weeks! In 1915 they set off for China together, having arranged to travel via Canada where my paternal grandparents had settled. Dorothy Rodwell wrote to her parents from Toronto in September 1915 a letter in which we can see the beginning of the change in his views: she wrote:

> "A remark of John's that he believed Christ came to fulfil and not destroy the best thought and ideals of every nation, created quite an interesting discussion, especially among the Hicksites."

On their return to Szechwan they came under the influence of Henry T. Hodgkin, who was much involved with the FFMA in China. Their experience came to mirror his as it is described in the Book of Discipline of the Society of Friends, which gives extracts of Friends' Faith and Practice (more fully in the 1959 edition, a shortened extract in the 1994 edition). When a young man, Henry Hodgkin had "some very profound religious experiences which meant much in shaping my life"; these made him:

> "so sure of the genuineness and value of one's own experience as to undervalue other types of experience. It is this which makes

eager missionaries or propagandists and it was as such that I went to China, still very sure of the 'greatness of the revelation' and but dimly aware that God, in his many-sided nature and activity was not one whit less manifest in ways and persons with which or with whom I could have little sympathy. I recognise (a change) to have taken place in myself, from a certain assumption that mine was really the better way, to a very complete recognition that there is no one better way, and that God needs all kinds of people whom I previously would have regarded as fit objects for my 'missionary zeal'".

These universalist beliefs, which were shared by my parents, were unacceptable to the more Evangelically minded Quaker missionaries and caused a considerable rift among FFMA workers in West China, bringing some bitterness into the relationships of colleagues. Gradually Dorothy and John Rodwell came to hold the view that loving service was more important than proselytising. For similar reasons in 1927 the Friends Foreign Mission Association was absorbed into the Friends' Service Council; this momentous change, of course, could not bring immediate rapprochement between missionaries who had such differing beliefs and priorities. Clashes of this kind and clashes of personality had been evident in West China for many years. At one time, certain Quakers were not on speaking terms with others. Paul exhorted the faithful,

> "to cast off the works of darkness and put on the armour of light; let us conduct ourselves becomingly as in the day ... not with quarrelling and jealousy". (Romans ch13vv12-14.)

Observant Chinese must have noted this large gap in the missionaries' armour and have allowed themselves a wry smile or, understandably, accused the Quakers of hypocrisy, and a lack of appreciation of our "inner dark" as well as of the "inner Light", so much emphasised by Friends. I am thankful to say that my parents never wrote in their letters and reports any negative criticism of their fellow Quakers and in later years told me that they had determined early in their married life that they would not harbour grudges. Not that they were, being human, without faults! But they tried to live close to "the leadings of love and truth" in a spirit of Christian forbearance. Though they did not speak openly of their inward spiritual life, except in ministry in Meetings for Worship, we knew that they were people of constant prayerfulness and a sustaining faith.

In reading the letters and Reports sent by FFMA missionaries to the China Committee in London, I am struck not by major faults revealed, but by their blindness and unacknowledged compromises. But who are we to judge? Future generations no doubt will see our blindness, our faults, hardly noticed by us. These missionaries of the early part of this century generally accepted many of the assumptions of their time, as we ourselves do, today. Most were proud of being British, many considered the British Empire an instrument of good in the world. They also came with their accepted social attitudes; my mother for example, in one of her first letters home from China wrote, "Everyone here travels by sedan chair", and when I read this I wondered how she could be oblivious of the fact that only a minority of Chinese could afford to travel in that way? The vast majority went on foot, or in towns by rickshaw, again if they could afford to do so. Our style of life was so very different from that of the ordinary Chinese; in Chengtu we lived in a large house in a compound with high walls enclosing gardens, croquet lawn and tennis court. There were over half-a-dozen servants, such as cook and kitchen helper (who might double as table-boy), cleaners, the children's nurse, gardener, the compound-gateman, and an odd-job man, one of whose duties was to empty the contents of our chamber pots and the indoor "mao fong". Thus our parents were freed up to do the teaching, preaching, medical and "extension work" for which the FFMA had sent them to China. The style in which we lived meant that socialising was with other Europeans or with the better-off Chinese. After the Communist revolution and the expulsion of the missionaries in 1949, our house was divided into six flats for Chinese families, which demonstrates the Chinese view of its size and potential.

In the very hot, humid summers the European women and children escaped to their cool bungalows in the surrounding hills, joined there by husbands as work permitted. These trips to the hills were great expeditions, involving a team of carriers for us in our sedan chairs and for the food and luggage. Margaret Simkin, an American Quaker, reporting on such a journey to the hills in 1924 writes that for herself alone:

> "I had four carriers on my chair, as a chair rides easier with four men than with three ... in addition there were three carriers to take my loads, each man carrying two baskets hung from shoulder poles."

61

The journey to the hills.
BY COURTESY OF THE
RODWELL FAMILY

As my mother with three blond, blue-eyed children, was carried past the villages on the way, followed by a procession of coolies carrying luggage and provisions, everyone came out to stare. Some of these villagers had most probably never been more than a few miles from home in their lives. We had a great time in the hills with so many other children to play with and our shared swimming pool. Such happy memories! Such a contrast with the later fears of the period of anti-Western feeling which followed. Chinese resentment against this anti-foreign feeling became specifically anti-British after the "Shanghai Incident" of 1925, "when British-officered soldiers in Shanghai fired on unarmed Chinese student demonstrators, killing ten of them and wounding fifty more".

We, with all other Szechwan foreign families, had to flee in junks down the river Yangtse; we travelled with the French consul and family and flew the French flag for our protection. Europeans, unlike their converts, were able to escape to safer areas, with the protection of their consuls, backed up by Treaties and ultimately by military force. "Gunboat diplomacy" meant exactly that; the Yangtse river basin was considered as a "sphere of British influence" and punishment by shelling from gunboats could be and on occasion, was inflicted on riverbank populations as reprisal for injury to British nationals, as occurred at Wanshien in 1926, where hundreds of Chinese were killed by several hours of bombardment from the river.

We may well ask what were the results of the many years that Quakers worked in China. At the time of the Cultural Revolution (1966) it seemed that the seeds that had grown to young plants had then been cut down. However it is too soon to tell what seeds have lain dormant and may yet prove fruitful. There are certain obvious legacies; for example the West China Union University has continued to flourish now as the Szechwan Medical College. Quakers joined with others to form an indigenous and ecumenical Protestant Christian body. We cannot know the long-term influence of the lives of many faithful Friends, strong in their religious beliefs and devoted to the well-being of the Chinese people. Writing of the expulsion or withdrawal of 13,000 British Protestant missionaries from China in the years 1949 to 1953, George Hood, a Presbyterian minister of long experience came to these conclusions:

"This was the end of 'China Missions', the biggest missionary enterprise of modern times. It came as the climax of an anti-foreign, anti-missionary and anti-imperialist movement which had developed over a hundred years. The basic failure had been that too many missionaries had not succeeded in identifying with those to whom they were sent."

That is of course, demonstrably true, and very sad. Nevertheless, there are gleams of light! For example when the city of Suining was in great danger in 1916 three Quakers, Henry Davidson, Leonard Wigham and John Rodwell acted as mediators between two warring armies; through their efforts, hostages were released and the city saved

John and Dorothy Rodwell, Mrs Wang, Henry, Joan(na), Phyllis and Ralph, 1926. Taken just before leaving Sichuan.
BY COURTESY OF THE
RODWELL FAMILY

from being looted and possibly burnt. Some of the prominent citizens waylaid them on their departure and expressed their gratitude in the presenting of embroidered scrolls to those they saw as the saviours of their city. Let these words, translations of the words of the scrolls, flowery but sincere, be their memorial:

> "You, in your kindness, have come across the Seas, and it has become well known here that you have your hearts full of the preaching of the Truth, and your widely displayed love has shown the true benevolence of your hearts. Regarding Righteousness as of great price, you have travelled far like pilgrims, fearing no danger, whether to the remotest East or the most deserted regions of the West. Since, in your hearts you have identified yourselves with all mankind, you are, in spite of the differences of our national customs, at one with us.

> When, within the last few years, you came to live with us at Suining, the inhabitants enjoyed peace as if we had partaken of good wine to repletion. But times changed and the beacons burned to warn the people. There was fighting over all the land so that we could not sleep in peace. Then you arose in your boldness, displaying hundredfold bravery.

> You and we, the people of Suining, helped one another. In sympathy with our hearts you went in and out among the combatants as a snake wriggles in its progress. Thus it came to pass that, without firing an arrow or casting a stone, they freed us from the danger that was impending.

> How we admire your action! Truly you may be styled righteous. Well may you be compared to Lu Lien, the hero of olden story. We, people of Suining, ponder on this and can never forget it, and so that the true perfume of the good deed may be preserved, we have written this record."

Dorothy and John Rodwell did not, unlike Clifford Stubbs (killed by Chinese in 1930), William Sewell and some other Friends' Service Council workers, return to China. I once asked my mother why? She said they thought it right to stay in England together, as a family, so as not to upset their children. John and Dorothy shared the Chinese ideals of the importance of the family - here are the words of the I Ching:

> "The family shows the laws operative within the household that, transferred to outside life, keep the state and the world in order. The foundation of the family is the relationship between

husband and wife. When the family is in order all the social relationships of mankind will be in order. The family is society in embryo: it is the native soil on which the performance of moral duty is made easy, through natural affection, so that within a small circle, a basis of moral practice is created, and this is later widened to include human relationships in general."

In 1926 our family with other foreigners, was forced to leave China through anti-British feeling. Over the ensuing years anti-Western attitudes grew, forcing the expulsion of almost all Europeans when the Communists took over mainland China in the 1940s. A great victory for the Chinese came during the Second World War when the Western European Allies agreed to give up all privileges they had obtained through the "unequal treaties" of years gone by. The Communist regime grew in strength in spite of the antagonism of the international community; and after many years of isolation, in 1971 the Peoples Republic of China was admitted to the United Nations organization. This was followed a year later by the state visit to the Peoples Republic of President Nixon of the United States. At last the Communist rulers felt able to relax some of the previous restrictions, and cautiously to open up the country. Sichuan and the far west of China had been totally forbidden to foreign visitors in these intervening years. In these distant areas some of the excesses of the Red Guards at the time of the Cultural Revolution were hidden from the outside world. We can only guess at the impact of all these upheavals on the members of the Society of Friends and other Christian churches in Sichuan during these momentous times.

In the early 1970s a few "foreign teachers" were appointed to work in China, among them Joanna Sutcliffe and my son Richard. In 1979 the authorities permitted a group of these teachers (who were already working in different parts of the country) to visit Chengtu. Joanna and Richard were among this first group allowed to visit Sichuan.

On the very day that they had departed from England they received a letter from me asking them to try to contact three people in Chengtu – Dr Fang, a Quaker, who had been a Fellow at Woodbrooke in his student days, and was well known to our family, Dr Stephen Yang of another Quaker family who were friends of my parents, and Liu Ch'ang Ch'eng, a childhood playmate.

When Joanna and Richard arrived in Chengtu, they had great difficulty in persuading the local Chinese officials to contact Dr Fang or anyone with former Quaker connections. Eventually, Dr Fang now elderly and not strong in health was brought to see them and in the

Jo and Richard's visit to Chengtu, 1979. From left: Liu Chang Ch'eng, Richard, Mary Yang, Jo and Stephen Yang.

course of conversation, remembered both Woodbrooke and his visits to our family in England.

Now I should explain that my son Richard is a geographer doing research into the growth of cities in China. So, in addition to asking to see Dr Fang he had as usual made his request to see the architect and planner of the city of Chengtu. While Dr Fang was still in the room this party arrived and on introductions being made with Dr Fang's help, it was suddenly apparent to my son that Mr Liu the architect was in fact Liu Ch'ang Ch'eng. That evening Joanna and Richard dined with the Liu family; Dr Stephen Yang was also present at this meal. So there they were, round the table with the very people they had been seeking to meet! And where was this supper held but in the kitchen of our former home in Green Dragon Street, which had been divided into six flats two of which were occupied by members of the Liu family.

What are we to make of these events? Do we conclude that they were just coincidences? Or do we agree with Archbishop William Temple's claim when he said "when I cease praying, coincidences do not happen" with the obvious inference that the opposite is also true? I am certain that the Chinese Quakers, cut off for so many years from British Friends had indeed both longed and prayed for renewed contact, which did indeed continue. Was this again the "ocean of light and love flowing over the ocean of darkness and death?"

CHINA AND FFMA

BOOKS CONSULTED

R.J. Davidson & Isaac Mason: *Life in West China*, Headley Bros., London, 1905.

J. Omerod Greenwood *Quaker Encounters*, Sessions, York.

  1 Friends and Relief (1975)

  2 Vines on the Mountains (1977)

  3 Whispers of Truth (1978)

William G. Sewell: *China Through a College* Window, Edinburgh House Press, London, 1937.

Han Suyin: *The Crippled Tree*, Panther Books Ltd., London, 1965.

Hilda Hookham: *A Short History of China*, Longmans, Green & Co. Ltd., London and Harlow, 1969.

Bette Bao Lord: *Spring Moon*, Victor Gollancz, London, 1981.

Henry Rodwell: *China Mission*, William Sessions, York, 1986.

Charles Tyzack: *Friends in China*, Sessions, York, 1988.

SOURCE MATERIALS

FFMA letters and reports from China, 1907 to 1927.

39th FFMA Annual Report and Review of Work *In Five Fields*, 1905/6.

Reports of Proceedings at FFMA Conferences 1892, 1895, 1907-1910.

All in the Library, Friends House, London.

The Darlington Conference of the FFMA *Our Foreign Missions* 1896, London, West Newman & Co., MDCCCXCVII.

Margaret Simkin: *Letters from Szechwan*, printed by Celo Press for the *Friend in the Orient Committee*, Pacific Yearly Meeting of the Religious Society of Friends, 1978.

Letters, reports and photographs in the possession of members of the Rodwell family, mainly John Rodwell, son of Henry Rodwell.

CHAPTER 10

FAMINE IN RUSSIA IN THE
1920s: QUAKER RELIEF

DURING the time my parents were in China momentous events were occurring in neighbouring Russia. In 1915, during the Great War the Germans had invaded Russia and a great number of refugees were forced to flee their homes. As ever in such circumstances food shortage was acute, water supplies polluted and scarce, and diseases such as typhoid and dysentery prevalent. The 1916 famine which followed was severe and a team of British and American Quakers was sent to help in any ways possible. Then came the 1917 Russia Revolution which exacerbated the plight of the refugees and the hungry and sick. Eventually the Quakers were forced to withdraw, a remnant remaining near Buzuluk until 1918. Since the formation of the International Red Cross in the mid nineteenth century, several war and disaster relief agencies have been founded, among them Save the Children, Christian Aid, Cafod and Oxfam (through a Quaker initiative in Oxford) and on a larger scale, the agencies of the League of Nations and later, of the United Nations. After the end of the First World War, those in the League of Nations concerned with relief began to appreciate that the Quakers, though a small society compared to others, had a contribution to make, particularly in Russia. Dr Fridtjof Nansen, the High Commissioner of the 'Comité International de Secours a la Russie' was reported in *The Friend* as saying of the Quakers:

"their foresight and their efforts had paved the way, as no other agency could have done, for an international effort to save millions of Russian people from starvation."

For their work in many countries especially from 1918 onwards, the Society of Friends became more widely known as ready to assist all suffering peoples impartially and to work for the overcoming and amelioration of the evils which accompany all wars. At the end of the Second World War, Quakers were very much engaged in relief work of differing kinds in many countries; this was their contribution, their way of trying to bring "light and love" to the "darkness and death", the hatred, violence and destruction caused by war. Friends sent teams of the Friends' Ambulance Unit and Friends Relief Service to the Middle East, China, India and the devastated areas of Europe, including Germany.

In John Punshon's words:

"They struggled to help displaced persons, collaborators, refugees, the destitute, the handicapped, the diseased and starving. They were a small part of the total effort of the relief services, but they were distinctive. In 1947 through its representative bodies, the American Friends Service Committee and the Friends Service Council of London, the Society of Friends was awarded the Nobel Peace Prize."

In making the presentation Gunnar Jahn spoke of Friends' witness for peace and opposition to the evils of war:

"It is not the positive political aspect of their activities which places Quakers in a special position. It is the silent help from the nameless to the nameless."

He went on to quote from the poet Arnulf Overland that Quakers and others doing such work "drew on the inexhaustible resources of the spirit".

And yet the members of the Quaker teams are not "nameless"; many are still remembered by Friends and others, particularly by those whom they helped, and we can read of them in different histories of Friends' relief work. A more recent description can be read in Bill Chadkirk's (1994) MA Thesis *Revolution and Relief* describing Quaker famine relief in the Samara province of Russia from 1916 to 1923.

There are two names in the account of Quaker relief in Russia which interest me particularly; Theodore Rigg and A.P.I. Cotterell. Theodore Rigg was a valuable team leader in Russia from 1915, and later became known among Friends as a prominent New Zealand Quaker and also as Director of the NZ Agricultural Research Institute in Nelson in the South Island. There, in addition to his job, he took a special interest in the life, work and death of John Sylvanus Cotterell, of which he wrote an account, valuable to me in my researches.

Albert Player Isaac Cotterell (1861-1951), to give him his full name was my grandmother's brother, one of a large family very active among West Country Friends. He is a representative Quaker of a kind not so frequently found today, for he had the financial means and the professional position which allowed him to offer for periods of Quaker service abroad. He trained as a Civil Engineer at Bristol University and became a specialist in water, drainage and sewerage problems. In 1920 he went to Russia to give advice and practical help to the team in the Buzuluk area to which Quakers had returned again. He was well qualified to advise on the water-borne diseases, such as cholera and typhoid and on the draining of the surrounding marshes where the malarial mosquito bred. There "API" (as he was usually called) and the Quaker team had some amazing experiences. *The Friend* of 6 January 1922 quotes from a letter written by A.P.I. Cotterell to the Friends Council for International Service of an encounter in Buzuluk in 1921, an extraordinary encounter indeed. He tells how among the refugees who had arrived in Buzuluk there was a group who called themselves "Quakers".

President – 1913
Albert P. I. Cotterell.

" Una Literas Didicimus."

SIDCOT OLD SCHOLARS' ASSOCIATION.

REPORT & PROCEEDINGS,
1913.

"We found that in their doctrinal beliefs and mode of worship they were just like ourselves, only they carry out their beliefs more literally",

based on their Bibles, which they all seemed to possess. They "see no need for outward form" and accept a:

"spiritual baptism. It is the same with Communion. They say they have no need to pay kopecks to the priest, for they all have equal access to God. In their meetings all are equal, and all have liberty to take part if moved by the Spirit."

They had tried to live out Christ's teachings in their lives. This had meant refusing military service, never killing living things, and therefore being vegetarians. Tom Copeman, another member of the team, amplifies API's account with further information:

"At that time the railway yards were packed with crowds of refugees waiting, often in vain, for transport. Among them Albert Cotterell to his great surprise one day encountered a group of people calling themselves Quakers."

Unfortunately API was called away to Moscow; in his absence some of these refugees came to tell the other two members of the advance party, Nancy Babb and Tom Copeman, that they had found transport and were leaving. They managed to have some time with them, speaking through an interpreter. Tom Copeman reported:

"We could not help being struck by their fine faces, especially the face of a matronly woman who sat with folded hands. They said they had always been called "Quakers" by other people, and according to tradition had been started '300 years ago by someone from England'".

They did not believe in taking oaths, nor in killing anything (even lice!); over 600 of them had refused military service under the late Czar and some had been imprisoned. They were released by the Soviet Government and were excused military service on condition that they registered in a commune for agricultural work.

"They registered their marriages with the Government but believed that in marriage they were guided by the Spirit and that registration or oath was unnecessary. For the purpose of marriage they held a Meeting when 'the brother declares to the sister that they will be married'. If matrimonial troubles arose a mature Friend was called in to give advice.

In the social order they seemed to be very near to Communism. In their religion they desired to be moved entirely by the Spirit and had no set forms. When a Meeting began they sang together or talked or sat in silence",

and they believed that the same Spirit of God was in them all, always.

"After we had finished our questions we had a short period of silence and they sang a hymn. It was a most wonderful experience and I felt very near to them and I think they to us."

As these "Quaker" refugees had to catch their train, they shook hands and departed with a box of clothing given by Friends. No more has ever been heard of this group, unfortunately, but there are now, again, a small number of Russians who are Quakers or connected with the Society of Friends. One of these, Sergei Nikitin, is now researching these earlier Quaker groups and the former presence of Quakers in Russia.

An article in *Quaker Life* of January/February 1998 by Sergei Nikitin entitled "Quakers and the Great Russian Famine" incorporates first-hand accounts from recipients of Quaker relief in Russia in the famine of 1921.

One example was the report of a Mrs Morozova "who remembered how when she was nine the Communist Red Army ran through their village Torpanovka like a gang of raiders, relieving civilians of all food supplies, horse and carts. Later, Quakers came to Torpanovka. They opened an orphanage in a church school for orphans and for those children whose parents were not able to feed them. Mrs Morozova said she was saved by Quakers, they gave her quinine when she was sick. She still remembers the food they were given: beans, rice, flour, chocolate and egg powder."

Sergei Nikitin researched archives in the Samara archives which reported that the Friends Relief Unit fed 397,723 people of the 478,772 that it was calculated needed food. "So, 83% of the local people were fed and saved by Quakers!"

"API" as he was often called, met Tolstoyans and other Russian pacifist groups, as well as Communists. There was a Famine Relief Committee of local sympathisers and notables who worked with Friends; the Quaker team also had a close connection with the "Save the Children Fund". At the height of the famine, the Quaker teams were providing food for 75,000 children and 100,000 adults (figure provided by Bill Chadkirk's Thesis). The publicity leaflets produced by Friends from Christmas 1921 appealed for funds to be sent to the Friends Relief Committee at 27 Chancery Lane. "The Friends have workers in the afflicted countries and the tales they have to tell would wring compassion from hearts of stone". In explaining the cause of the famine it went on "There are contributory causes – chiefly caused by seven years of foreign and civil war; also the grain requisitions made during that period for feeding the urban population in other parts of Russia."

A later appeal reassured some considering whether to contribute or not, that "The Friends' long experience is a guarantee of the wise expenditure of money entrusted to their care... The food trucks are sealed at the Russian frontier and opened in the presence of Quaker workers. The food goes direct, therefore to the sufferers".

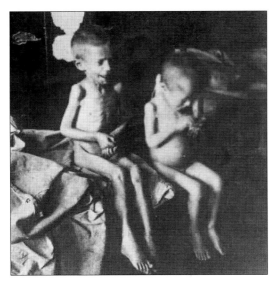

Hospital for famished children, Russia c1922.
BY COURTESY OF
FRIENDS HOUSE LIBRARY

At home in Britain an All-British Appeal Fund was set up in 1921, which was supported by all the political parties, the Archbishops and other religious leaders; this meant that medical supplies, food, clothing, seed-corn and fodder could be purchased for distribution. The American Relief Administration was altogether a bigger provider of food and other necessities in certain areas; but the English Quakers had the advantage of being a more flexible body with personal contacts from previous work in the region of Buzuluk. They were able to buy grain, fodder for the horses and cattle, as well as horses and camels for transport. Nevertheless, in spite of all relief efforts the situation in the Buzuluk area was dire; famine and disease such as cholera, malaria, tuberculosis and typhus caused so many deaths that skeletal corpses could be seen piled up awaiting burial. Tom Copeman wrote of conditions in Buzuluk as being like the descriptions in Daniel Defoe's *Journal of the Plague Year*, with the mournful sound of the tolling of bells for funerals and the gruesome sight of the death-carts, collecting unburied corpses from the streets and from the institutions for orphan and abandoned children.

In October 1921 in a letter to Cuthbert Clayton API added that his typewriter was again functioning "I have got it fixed up with string and a match end for a screw. We have no repairer or spare parts here".

He reports on visits with Nancy Babb (another Quaker worker) to Maternity Homes and the Children's Hospital, to which they took Quaker supplies. They found the wards clean, with enough clothing provided but the beds were scantily covered....many sick children in some cases terribly wasted by hunger." The two Maternity Homes they visited "were some of the saddest places I have ever been in." One was known as "the house of death, but the other is, if anything, worse, with for example 30 to 40 babies lying in rows on the floor covered by a single rag (I couldn't call it a sheet), most of them wailing piteously". Three to four of these babies die daily out of a total of about one hundred and thirty.

On his return to England, Albert Cotterell spoke to Friends and others about the terrible conditions in Russia in the 1921/22 famine areas. He addressed many meetings; for example London Young Friends were much concerned and called a meeting where he was to speak. The Friend publicised the situation, for,

> "The immensity of the need is scarcely appreciated by the average Englishman, and if ignorance is to be translated into knowledge and apathy into sympathy, it is essential that those who are seeking to work in the cause of humanity be equipped with a knowledge of the facts of the situation."

And funds and gifts did flow in to the Friends Emergency and War Victims Committee, not only from the members of the Society of Friends but from many members of the public, some Trade Unions and many notable individuals. There were some, even among Friends, who objected to sending aid to the "murdering Bolsheviks"; and the British Government kept up its policy of blockade against revolutionary Russia.

According to his obituary (in *The Friend* 1952) API Cotterell hoped that he personally as well as other Friends "should act as a bridge between pacifism and communism." In this same spirit, he became Clerk of the Committee set up by Meeting for Sufferings in 1926 "to see conciliation between owners and miners during the General Strike; he and other Friends made contact with miners and their leaders", we are not told with what result, if any. But at least the attempt at mediation was made.

"API" had useful specialist knowledge, was public-spirited in his work as a local councillor in Bristol and later as chairman of Jordans Village Ltd, and in his involvement with the Adult School movement. His time at Sidcot Friends' School meant a great deal to him and he was the President in 1913 of the Sidcot Old Scholars Association. His

Presidential Address is eloquent and moving; he recalled his school-days and the friends he made then with affection. He spoke of the influence of the school in "wakening ideals and principles which never all our lives long entirely forsake us". "API" had a deep appreciation of the beauty of the Sidcot valley and the surrounding hills, which "have aroused in many a love for Natural History and for Art" and which inspired him to write poetry. Not only was he "an authority in his profession" but had enough income and time to give himself to voluntary work. He was a dedicated Friend and gave service in many spheres: in 1938 he visited both Syria and Palestine on behalf of Friends and there he "refused armed escort during that dangerous time", for he was a staunch upholder of the Friends Peace Testimony. Later he visited Holland and Germany on behalf of Friends. He was a man of "integrity and unswerving principle", yet is also described as being "good company, friendly, and could see a joke". His contributions to the Cotterell family magazine, *The Swallow* (named after "Swallowcliffe" where they lived) reveals API as a man of broad interests in Nature, in all religions and the many diverse forms of Christianity as well as in many kinds of philanthropic endeavours. All his action, public and private, was founded on his inner devotional life and on his faithful membership of the Society of Friends. He was regular in attending Meetings for Worship, business meetings, also Yearly Meetings. Towards the latter part of his life he returned to live in Jordans and helped to restart the Meeting. The Testimony continues:

> "his eloquence and welcoming smile, together with his fervour in prayer and ministry will long be remembered there."

All these reports make API seem a paragon of Quaker virtues; however, in the "Testimony to the Grace of God" in his life another side of API is, unusually, mentioned:

> "He was a man of very definite views, and could not tolerate inefficiency and slackness, which sometimes made him show understandable impatience."

Since Friends tend to follow the maxim "speak no ill of the dead" those words can be understood as meaning that API was not always an easy man to get along with!

As I remember my great-uncle on his visits to us, he was a tall, big-built man of imposing manner, a contrast to his petite sister, my grandmother. I wish that I had been old enough to enquire from him, his first-hand impressions of his time in Russia. His deep faith had inspired him to join the Friends Relief Unit at a time of revolution and famine;

there, working together with Russians and other agencies, the Friends brought practical help, "light and love", to places of "darkness and death".

BOOKS CONSULTED

A. Ruth Fry: *A Quaker Adventure: the Story of nine years Relief and Reconstruction*, Nisbet & Co., 1926.

J. Ormerod Greenwood: *Quaker Encounters*, Vol. I *Friends and Relief*, Sessions of York, 1975.

Richenda C. Scott: *Quakers in Russia*, Michael Joseph, 1964.

Bill Chadkirk MA: Thesis *Revolution and Relief*, 1994.

PRIMARY SOURCES

Articles contributed to "The Swallow", the Cotterell family magazine (courtesy of Patricia Frood, née Cotterell) by A.P.I.

Presidential address to Ackworth Old Scholars, printed in the A.O.S.A. Magazine in 1913.

From the archives in Friends House Library:

Correspondence between A.P.I. Cotterell and Cuthbert Clayton.

Letters of Tom Copeman.

Article giving an account of the famine in the Samara district in *The Friend* of 29 July 1921.

Letter of appreciation of the work of the Friends Relief Committee from Fridtjof Nansen, 23 September 1921.

Letters from A.P.I. to the Friends War Victims Relief Committee.

Letter from A.P.I. to Joan Fry from Riga, August 1921.

Letter from A.P.I. to Ruth Fry, September 1921.

Minutes and Reports of the Friends Emergency Committee.

Minutes and Reports of the Friends War Victims Relief Committee.

Obituary of A.P.I. in *The Friend*, 4 January 1952.

Yearly Meeting Testimony to the Grace of God in the life of Albert P.I. Cotterell, 1953.

Theodore Rigg: *Chronicle of a Relief Worker in Buzuluk*.

CHAPTER 11

FRIENDS SERVICE COUNCIL: A SLOW CHANGE

IN the twentieth century, where the Society of Friends was known at all outside their own membership, it was in the fields of social reform and later, of war relief work, as the presentation of the Nobel Peace Prize in 1947 demonstrates. Nevertheless Quakers were active in less high-profile ways, for example in their quiet work in India. The century began with most Friends who were working abroad, doing so under the auspices of the Friends Foreign Mission Association. For example, Geoffrey Maw, when working for Friends in India, reluctantly had to accept the missionary label "because there was no other". However, as I have described, under the leadership of Henry T. Hodgkin and those who shared his views, a subtle change began within and towards the Friends Foreign Mission Association; there were new aims "far removed from mere proselytisation". From 1927 when the FFMA, the Council for International Services and some other Quaker bodies amalgamated to form the Friends Service Council, there was an accelerated rate of change where the emphasis was on "service".

The Friends Service Council became responsible for all relief and development work abroad on behalf of the Society, with no declared aim of continuing the evangelical, missionary work of the FFMA. From the 1930s onward, those who were sent abroad on Quaker work expected to be co-workers with those they had come to help and support. No longer were they to be considered as bringing light to those in darkness from a morally superior position.

My sister, Phyllis Short has sent me from her home in New Zealand, an interesting account which illustrates this change. Her husband Joe Short came from a farming background in New Zealand, and was trained there in horticulture, with further training in Kew Gardens and the State Botanic Gardens in Berlin. There he met Quakers, including Gwen and Corder Catchpool, also Muriel Lester and her niece Dorothy Hogg, who had just come from India where they had travelled with Gandhi on his "Untouchable Campaign". Phyllis writes:

"Well, Joe was completely blown away by the atmosphere and the meeting for worship."

He returned to England just before the Second World War, joined the Society of Friends, and having been inspired by reading Stanley Jones' *Christ of the Indian Road* and Gandhi's *Experiments With Truth*, offered to the FSC to go to India. He was sent for preparation to Woodbrooke and Kingsmead, where he met my sister Phyllis, who was living at Woodbrooke while training as a Primary School teacher. Phyllis told me of her own sense of 'mission' after hearing Gwen Catchpool speak at the Mount School. Joe, being a New Zealander was not conscripted for war service and arrived in India in 1941 to take over a Quaker land settlement scheme and village of Makoriya, as Heinz Tucher, previously in charge, had been interned as an enemy alien. After three years, on Heinz' return on parole, Joe went on to Rasulia where Donald and Erica Groom were working on Gandhian lines. Meanwhile in 1944, Phyllis had arrived and six days later, they were married. They stayed at Rasulia, where she writes:

"it was a lovely pattern of living. In the morning we had silent meditation like worship, and spinning in the Gandhian style. And Joe and I had lessons in Hindi".

While at Rasulia, Phyllis was involved in Gandhian Basic Schools. At the beginning of 1945 they visited Gandhi in his Ashram of Sevagram, where he lived in a simple village-style house of packed mud. She continues:

"When we got to the ashram and were invited to attend the evening prayers that very evening, there he was sitting ... We sat there in a big circle with the Ashram members and Gandhi, a little space between him and other people, and we had evening prayers, the readings from the Scriptures of Islam, Hinduism and Christianity. This evening it was from the Koran ... Actually at this prayer meeting a small child, a real crawling age child, started in his lap then was climbing up round one shoulder, climbing up the other shoulder, and he just patted this child and spoke when he had something to say, and so on. I, fresh from England looked and thought 'where is this child's mother? How could they allow this child to bother the great man?' Later I realised it was rather like a story I knew from the Bible! And you can just see your own conditioning, it's so extraordinary. He was perfectly happy and the little child was happy too."

Later when they were both invited to visit him in his house there was another echo of a New Testament story.

"Gandhi asked me as his first question to me, 'Can you speak Hindi?' I'd been in the country less than a month. I said 'No, but I'm learning'. He said 'You'll be no use without it' and roared with laughter. He was having me on really. Which made me realise that in the gospels Jesus had people on. Think about that woman, from Samaria. You know, he talked about how he came there only for the Jews, and she said 'But the dogs can eat the crumbs from under the table.' A beautiful bit of repartee and I thought how stupid we are about all this when obviously they were joking. Jesus must have been a very charismatic and humorous person and I saw glimmerings of that in meeting Gandhi."

Phyl and Joe then went on to visit Santineketan, where it came as a shock after the simplicity of Gandhi's life, to find the opulence of Rabindranath Tagore's former home. This had become a pioneering centre of Indian culture, Indian dance, Indian music, Indian art and literature. In honour of the much respected C.F. Andrews, there was also a house for the study of Christian thought. Two miles away was the village of Sriniketan, "the abode of plenty" where Tagore had

Phyllis Mary Short (neé Rodwell)
b.1921.

Joseph Godfrey Short
b.1916 d.1982.

BY COURTESY OF THE RODWELL FAMILY

79

started his experiment in rural renewal. Joe was asked to manage the model farm and dairy and orchard there by Leonard Elmhurst (well known for the founding of Dartington Hall School) who was funding a good deal of this work. In 1946 Joe with Phyl and baby Michael removed to Santiniketan, where they lived in a staff house, moving to Sriniketan a year later. They were asked then by the Gandhian Basic Education people for help in preparing a curriculum for older children on the growing of food and care of the land.

> "That was right in Joe's line ... and he and I wrote a curriculum for older Indian children based on their rural lives."

By 1949 the family had moved on to the Agricultural Institute at Allahabad where Joe worked in the horticulture and extension departments.

> "There were also Hindu and Muslim students ... It was a place where everybody worked together and talked to each other and made friends."

As Joe wrote when first going to India:

> "The agricultural and economic problem must be tackled right from the bottom, the soil itself, and not only with Christians but with all."

In the attempt to introduce better cultivation methods and new crops the Institute trained "Village-Level" workers, which was part of Joe's work.

> "He also travelled around, giving practical advice to missions which had land, on landscaping and land use."

By then there were three children in the family, with whom Phyllis was occupied, especially as they were taught by her at home through the New Zealand Correspondence School. She was also involved in a school for healthy children of leprosy patients, run by the Mission of Lepers, nearby.

In all the experiences of their life in India and their sympathy with Gandhi and willingness to work with and to learn from people of a different culture and religious faith, what could be further away from the old style missionary approach? Phyllis writes:

> "Surely 'serving God by serving humankind' is not missionary endeavour, it is being alongside people and working with them towards solving their problems whether they are growing more food (Joe) or learning to understand their culture and themselves through education (me, in Basic Schools for example)

Phyllis and Joe with baby in Indian dress.
BY COURTESY OF THE
RODWELL FAMILY

and in the process, sharing the deeper things mutually ... We did not go to make Christians or Quakers".

Do not all the major religions of the world share the same basic tenets? I have recently been dipping into *A Dictionary of Religious and Spiritual Quotations* compiled by Geoffrey Parrinder. It is plain that the ancient Indian scriptures give similar teaching to the Bible; and the Mahatma Gandhi's words and actions reflect those of Jesus.

As John Woolman wrote in 1762 (extract 26.61 of *Quaker Faith and Practice* Revised edition 1994):

> "There is a principle which is pure, placed in the human mind, which in different places and ages hath different names; it is however, pure and proceeds from God. It is deep and inward, confined to no forms of religion nor excluded from any where the heart stands in perfect sincerity. In whomsoever this takes root and grows, of what nation soever, they become brethren".

And of course, sisters.

FRIENDS SERVICE COUNCIL: INDIA

BOOKS CONSULTED

Martha Dart: *To Meet at the Source: Hindus and Quakers*, Pendle Hill pamphlet No. 289, 1989.

Martha Dart: *Marjorie Sykes, Quaker Gandhian*, Sessions, York, 1993.

Arun Gandhi: *Daughter of Midnight: Child Bride of Gandhi*, Blake Publishing, 1998.

J. Ormerod Greenwood: *Vines on the Mountain & Whispers of Truth*, Sessions, York, 1977 and 1978.

Bede Griffiths: *Marriage of East and West*, Harper Collins, 1983.

Geoffrey Parrinder: *A Dictionary of Religious and Spiritual Quotations*, Simon & Schuster, 1989.

Marjorie Sykes: *An Indian Tapestry: Quaker Threads in the History of India, Pakistan and Bangladesh, from the 17th Century to Independence*, ed. Geoffrey Carnall, Sessions Book Trust, York,1997.

SOURCE MATERIAL

An Oral history of New Zealand Friends, taken by Penelope Dunkley.

Transcript of above with additional information in letters etc. from Phyllis Short of Auckland, New Zealand.

PART TWO: THE PRESENT

CHAPTER 12

CLARIFICATION

WHEN my husband was a child he was for a time, looked after by a young girl who to rebuke him would say "Wachermeanbyit?" which he thought was one word. So before I go any further it would be as well to clarify some of the meanings I give to certain words, so as to prevent any misunderstanding. The word "God" is a turn-off for many, especially if they have had an upbringing in some of the churches where the idea of "God somewhere out there", watching all we do in a judgmental and punitive spirit has been instilled. I use the word simply as shorthand for the Spirit within and throughout, that in which "we live and move and have our being", "The Ground of our Being, the Numinous, the Ultimate Reality, the Creative Intelligence", indeed the most mysterious and indescribable. I never think of Him/She/It as an old man with a white beard sitting above the earth on a cloud! I do think of this "Ultimate Reality" as having a personal aspect - otherwise how could we have "that of God" within us, or have the possibility of communion with this "God"? A common form of address to God over the centuries has been "Lord". This appellation is both feudal and patriarchal, but we cannot rewrite the Scriptures nor hymns and prayers to suit our modern sensibilities. As Advice No. 17 suggests:

> "When words are strange or disturbing to you try to sense where they come from".

Jesus is to me, a Jewish holy man and prophet, filled with the love of God, so filled that he is indeed the "son of God"; but we too, are sons and daughters of God, each of us with a measure of the same Holy Spirit that filled Jesus. "Christ" means for me the eternal, universal Light, the Holy Spirit in all people.

84

"Spirit" is again, something almost impossible to describe, but even children can feel and know whether someone addresses them or treats them in a loving or an angry and inimical spirit. We all recognise this in our own experience. I love the story in John (chap 4 v24) of Jesus' encounter with the woman of Samaria at the well: "God is spirit and those who worship him must worship in spirit and in truth"; I prefer to leave out the "him" as I cannot accept even the symbolic idea of a male or female "God". I share with a friend, a Ghanaian, his experience that when he read of the life and faithfulness to death of Jesus, his heart burned within him. As regards the Bible, chiefly in the New Testament, we read words and of deeds which resonate in us; this is not by a literal acceptance of these writings but a recognition that "the letter killeth but the spirit giveth life". Jesus taught that to live a life of true spirituality we should "love God and love our neighbours as ourselves". When we ignore these injunctions, this is wrongdoing (i.e. sin) which brings the opposite of good (i.e. evil) as a direct or indirect result.

Love is again a very difficult word because it is used with quite different meanings, for example there is sentimental love, sexual love, love of children, of family and of friends. Paul gives a wonderful description of the true form of love in 1 Corinthians Chapter 13, which cannot be bettered. The First Letter of John has this to say "love is of God, and he who loves is born of God and knows God, for God is love" (I John chapter 4 vv7-12). (We today would prefer an inclusive expression, but need to remember that in past years "man" was used for "humankind" and meant both male and female.)

Religion is usually used today to denote an institution with dogma and creeds. Many Quakers now prefer to use the word spirituality, meaning the Inner Light in all. Likewise the adjective spiritual is often preferred to the adjective religious. I have always understood both religion and spirituality as descriptions of faith; I am happy with the Chamber's Dictionary definition of religion as "belief in, recognition of, or an awakened sense of a higher unseen controlling power or powers with the emotion and morality connected therewith" (though I would query the concept "controlling", and "powers" in the plural).

John Hick in his *Evil and the God of Love* quotes Keats, that on this earth we are in a "vale of soul-making", but Hick admits that he has no answer for the extreme and unmerited suffering of some people, particularly of children. Since we are social animals, it follows that the innocent will suffer with the guilty even from one generation to the next, for we are all bound up together. The doctrine of Free Will has no answer to explain the terrible results and suffering caused by natural disasters such as earthquakes, cyclones and flood. We are told by some "process" theologians and scientists that such disasters are inevitable in an evolving universe. In past centuries the Devil was blamed for calamities and both personal and general evils. Satan, the Evil One, is to me, simply a human personification, a projection of our Inner Dark. As for disease, accident, inherited human problems where the innocent suffer, we have no answers. This is life as we find it and have to accept it.

We long to be saved from evil, from human cruelty, falsehood, stupidity, from "death and darkness" in all its forms. "To be saved" is usually described as "Salvation", and the orthodox Christian teaching in that Salvation comes from Jesus' death on the cross. I find William Tynedales's translation (1525) of Salvation as "health" more interesting and helpful. Even more intriguing is the Gospel of the ancient Syrian church where:

"to save" is given as "to live"

"Salvation" is given as "life"

"Saviour" is given as "Life-giver".

(I owe this information to Hugh McGregor Ross in his Introduction to the Gospel of Thomas.)

CHAPTER 13

MY LIFE - EXPERIENCE

A LL those whose lives I have described so far (except perhaps the Wakefield brothers) considered themselves to be witnesses to the Truth and to the love of God, seeing themselves as disciples of Jesus Christ. They longed to share their experiential faith, the good news, the 'gospel', with others. They cared about all those they met, even their opponents, seeking to respond to "that of God" within the most unlikely, sometimes hostile people.

As Elizabeth Fry states so clearly in her *Journal*, she found it essential to "practise the presence of God" by private prayer, by the reading of the Scriptures and by her faithful attendance at Friends Meetings for Worship; these were the means for receiving "daily strength for daily needs". I knew this discipline to be a regular practice too, in my parents' lives.

All knew full well that they were up against the dark side of human life, which early Friends described as evil, the work of the Devil; they knew too, that they were called to overcome evil by good, so that the darkness might be flowed over by light and love. And yet, from the Yearly Meeting minutes of 1690 we learn that Quaker children were to be protected from ungodly influences, to be given a "guarded education" at school as well as at home. These children were to learn to "walk in the Light" without, if possible, experiencing the dark. How then, were they expected to deal with the dark side of themselves and with the darkness in the world?

I now turn to my own experience of a 'guarded' upbringing and education and the results in my own life.

My parents, of whom I have already written (see China chapter) were thoughtful, loving Quakers, neither solemn nor censorious, but Quakers with a good sense of humour and of fun, with an ability to enjoy life. I was the second of their four surviving children, and had a happy and cared for childhood, which I took for granted as a normal state.

My parents shared an unspoken devotion to the tenets of the New Testament, for example in following the advice of Paul in his letter to the Philippians (Ch4v8):

> "Finally, brethren, whatsoever things are true, whatsoever things are honest, whatsoever things are just, whatsoever things are pure, whatsoever things are lovely, whatsoever things are of good report; if there be any virtue, and if there be any praise, think on these things."

So there was no morbid dwelling on tragedies, disasters or human wrongdoing. We read the *News Chronicle* so were aware of both national and world events, but we never saw the tabloid press with its emphasis chiefly on scandals, horrors and anything at all sensational which could make an arresting headline. In our home there was virtually no gossip of any kind, particularly not any malicious gossip; my father was not very interested in such matters, had other concerns on his mind, my mother was interested in people, but both took seriously the Biblical injunction not to speak ill of others, and if they could not speak well of somebody, they chose to say nothing. With the emphasis on the Inner Light in all human beings which was assumed at home, at Meeting for Worship and later at a Friends School, I grew up with an unrealistic appreciation of the motivations and behaviour of many of our fellow human beings. We took it for certain that the Inner Light could be appealed to, in all human relationships. And were we not advised to "know one another in that which is eternal"? So I had little understanding of the dark side of all human beings and had no inkling that I, myself, when hard pressed, could harbour very unQuakerly feelings and responses to others! So, through later experiences in life, I had some hard lessons to learn. In my earlier years I had had no need to "dig within" for the strong and terrible emotions and impulses which are described by Shakespeare and other writers, for there was nothing more serious than some sibling jealousy, little in my family or environment to arouse the inner demons which are present in us all. I suspect I was both naive and priggish.

As a family we attended a Friends' Meeting for Worship regularly wherever we were living. When young, we children attended the Children's classes, where we were told stories from the Bible or from Quaker history, and as we grew older a *Book of Quaker Saints* and *Paul the Dauntless* were read to us by different adults from the Meeting. At home mother read to us frequently, beginning as I recall, with fairy stories, the Beatrix Potter stories of *Peter Rabbit, Mrs Tiggywinkle* and the *Tailor of Gloucester,* Kipling's *Just So Stories* and the *Jungle Books,* some ballads and poetry. Not for some years did I realise the quiet censorship mother exercised; we never heard read the more unusual and frightening Beatrix Potter stories of the wicked Fox's doings, for example, and certain lines in the ballads were subtly altered as she read, so as to omit swearing and unpleasantness. Ralph the Rover did more than "beat his breast in his despair" which was the version mother read to us - he "curs'd himself in his despair!"

After our return from China, when at last we were settled in Derby, I was sent to a private school run by a Mrs Baker and attended by a small number of well-behaved middle-class boys and girls. We were well-taught by Mrs Baker on the Parents' National Educational Union scheme; she was a kindly, intelligent woman and I remember her with affection. In 1932, at the age of twelve, I followed my older brother to the Friends' School, Saffron Walden in Essex.

So, at home I had lived in a protected environment - though not as protected as some Roman Catholic girls I knew, whose father cut photos and articles out of the daily paper before the family was permitted to see it. In these days of television in almost every home is such "protection" possible, I wonder? The Friends' School at Saffron Walden also attempted to give the pupils a "guarded education". We brought books from home for our own reading but these had to be censored, passed as suitable by the headmistress at the beginning of term; magazines and books not submitted for inspection were confiscated. On Saturday evenings the headmistress had all the girls gathered together for her to read improving literature to us, while we busied our hands in our 'fancywork', usually knitting or embroidery. We were read many of the *Pollyanna* series, about the little girl who saw the good in everything with a total optimism; we heard also the semi-autobiographical novel *Jeremy* by Hugh Walpole, and when Miss Priestman came to a swear word she would say "'Bad word' said Jeremy", then read on. We had no contact with the people of the town, nor with the town children except for a few day-scholars. Once a week, when granted permission and in twos, we were allowed to spend our pocket-money in local shops, but that was the only permitted contact, unless we were invited to tea with a known household, or taken out by visiting relatives. Nevertheless, having a number of children from Nazi Germany in the school, we could not be totally protected from

The author, aged 22 years.

knowledge of the outside world, for we heard their stories and of the events which made them refugees.

What was the aim of this "guarded" Quaker upbringing and education? I find myself very puzzled by this question. Was the aim to build up Quaker character which would stand firm in the trials of life, relying on faith, to do so? As far as my brother and I were concerned, our background led to a quite unrealistic and over-optimistic expectation of the world and of people, which could lead only to disillusion, almost to nervous breakdown, as happened to my brother on his first contact with working men on the 'shop' floor. My supervisor in my first job was a sharp-tongued and hypercritical woman, who reduced me to tears very quickly, for I had never met such treatment and had no idea how to cope. It may well be that for some of my fellow-Quakers of a similar background, with just such a sheltered upbringing and Friends' School education, this led as it did for me, to passivity in the face of domineering behaviour, unwillingness to make hard decisions and a taking of the course of least resistance which may ultimately involve the condoning of wrong actions. Did these traits affect the Society of Friends as a body in the recent past, when so many came from Quaker homes and had attended Quaker schools I wonder?

I think, for myself, I believed, without being consciously aware of this, that to be both Quaker and pacifist meant to be passive. When later, in my adult life I was brought into close contact with people who had very different attitudes and goals in life, some who wished to dominate or were unkind, I struggled to deal with them in a Quakerly way, but with little success. I do remember telling my troubles to my mother, who answered that I should make plain that certain behaviour was hurting me, and it would then stop. It did not stop, but increased; some time passed before I came to realise that some people actually enjoy hurting others. So how should a true Quaker respond? The social reformer John Bellers (of whom I have written) had no doubt at all. He believed with all the early Friends, that "standing still in the Light", obeying the Inward Teacher and so living close to God, it was possible to live in a loving and Christlike spirit. In his pamphlet on *Anger and Perturbations* he wrote of anger as unQuakerly, unChristian, as a sin to be overcome, supporting his view by quotations from the Old and New Testaments.

At one period of my life I came under extreme pressure; to my amazement, horror and fear I found myself full of not only great anger but hatred, a desire to hurt in revenge, horrible feelings. In my distress

I prayed for help; I confided in Quaker friends but my circumstances were not understood and the simple remedies offered were of no avail. I turned for help to our *Christian Life Faith and Thought in the Religious Society of Friends* and the companion volume Christian Practice. The negative emotions which were tearing me apart were not even in the index. Having tried unsuccessfully to cope I fled the situation, feeling guilty and a failure by the Quaker standards of my upbringing. I have had to come to terms with my dark side; such shattering experiences had revealed aspects of myself previously hidden from me. I looked back and saw that growing up as a Quaker and remaining a member of the Society had kept me in a cosy nest from which I could look out at the world but feel personally uninvolved in its cruelties, and where in Meeting for Worship I could feel a sense of peace. It is not possible to continue to live at such a superficial level once you have encountered what Jung calls the "shadow"; this is all to the good, for however painful, facing the truth about ourselves is ultimately liberating and can lead to healing and a degree of wholeness.

For some years I felt such a sense of failure in my personal life that I could not for example, share in the Friends' Peace Testimony. If I could not love those I knew, people close to me, how could I claim to love my enemies? Is not this kind of love, loving those who "despitefully use" us the difficult love which is demanded of us if we claim to be pacifist? Is common sense, our rationality, even our belief in "that of God" in friend and foe alike, enough? I have come to believe that to attempt such difficult loving is "in right ordering", even if we have failed and may well fail again. William Penn expressed this in 1693:

> "Love is the hardest lesson in Christianity; but, for that reason, it should be more our care to learn it." (Q.F. & P. Extract 22.01)

My views on anger have changed over the years. Observation of my own and others' children has shown me that as humans, we are born ready to be angry. This is a necessity for survival: babies will yell with frustration if their needs and wishes are not met promptly. In some adults a similar reaction is near to the surface; family and colleagues are aware of this and usually try not to cross them. Others live with deep, hidden, suppressed anger which is liable to come out at a totally unexpected time and in an unwarranted manner, perhaps triggered by an unrelated event even by a trivial happening. As a Friend said to be once, "If you swallow anger you swallow it alive"! I suspect that this tends to result from a controlled, often a middle-class upbringing; though my mother's considered judgement as she once told me, was that deliberate, conscious self-control was very different from repression by the subconscious self.

But we need to be aware of living in a hostile spirit, with anger ever ready to erupt for *The Journal of the American Medical Association* (2000; 283; 2546-51) as quoted in *Health Which* Research Bulletin for March 2001, warns "People who are prone to anger have an increased risk for heart disease and death".

During the Second World War, for some months I helped to look after some small evacuees from Hull, who had no social inhibitions about expressing their jealousy, anger or any other such emotion. I well remember the shock I received when I had to separate two very small children who were fighting over a particular toy. They were clawing at each other's faces, drawing blood, and as the noise grew louder, their mothers came banging on the playroom door, taking sides and starting to bash each other on their children's behalf, for they also, had few inhibitions about expressing any emotion, positive or negative. For someone brought up to exercise control over the expression of such feelings, as I was, this was a great shock. John Bellers and the Quakers who thought as he did and those Friends who share his views today would be totally disapproving of such behaviour. Some few can rise above such negative emotions, some have so great a measure of the Light that they are enabled to live in a loving and tolerant manner. This is what George Fox proclaimed when he told the Commonwealth Commissioners that he:

> "lived in the virtue of that life and power that took away the occasion of all wars ... I told them I had come into the covenant of peace which was before wars and strife were". (Q.F. & P. Extract 24.01)

Many of us, myself included, have to struggle on, admitting to our feelings, apologising to any we have injured in our anger and learning to bear with our own shortcomings and to walk in "the measure of Light" that we have. Having forgiven ourselves where we were at fault, the next step is forgiveness of the others involved, leading at best, to reconciliation. All these steps can be painful and difficult. In South Africa, Nelson Mandela and Desmond Tutu have led the process of Truth and Reconciliation, giving a shining example to us all, of the power of truthful confession, forgiveness and reconciliation! Nevertheless, as with "righteous indignation", anger can give us the necessary energy to stand up for ourselves where it is right to do so; to oppose injustice, oppression and all manner of evils.

Over the years I have learned much from some feminists and peace activists (I especially remember a Peace Week at Woodbrooke in the 1980s); I have learned that it is essential to be honest with oneself and with others too: to challenge small things going wrong and not to "Gunny-sack" them until the sack is full to overflowing, in the mistaken belief that Christians should as Paul wrote "bear all things, endure all things" in silence. I remember trying to "bear all things", then one more thing to bear was one thing too much and I would blow off like a volcano! To learn to "speak the truth in love" rather than keeping silence for "peace" is very demanding, a lesson I am still trying to learn. To speak truth as a weapon, in anger or disapproval is not so hard: "to speak the truth in LOVE" is one of the harder things we are called upon to do, and for me this kind of honest and loving confrontation is taking a lifetime of learning.

At Woodbrooke again, I have found great help in coming to terms with the dark as well as the light in my nature, in the workshops run by Brenda Heales and Chris Cook of the "Appleseed Project". Expressing oneself in paint or clay or in worship-sharing has been wonderfully releasing and healing for me. In contrast to earlier editions our Quaker Faith and Practice (1994 Revised Edition) has many references to the dark side of ourselves, our intolerance, our blindness, our lack of love, often our hostility which we may deny.

I am thankful too, that in the 1994 edition of our Advices and Queries we are given a vision of the possibility of good in ourselves and in others and of the transforming power of the Meeting for Worship, where, as Robert Barclay found, the evil in us may be weakened and the good raised up. Number 10 and number 11 speak of the dark as well as of the light:

> "Come regularly to meeting for worship even when you are angry, depressed, tired or spiritually cold." (no. 10)

> "Be honest with yourself. What unpalatable truths might you be evading? When you recognise your shortcomings, do not let that discourage you. In worship together we can find the assurance of God's love and the strength to go on with renewed courage." (no. 11)

When we are not honest with ourselves nor in our dealings with others, relationships cannot flourish. In my life and observation, forgiveness is the key to reconciliation and the making of a new beginning. Joyfulness, enthusiasm (meaning literally "inspiration from God"), a good sense of humour and laughter too, are all infectious and can help to bring "love and light" to many dark and difficult personal situations. Nevertheless we must respect the feelings and decisions of those who have endured extreme forms of suffering at the hands of others. Rabbi Hugo Gryn has made clear that "as a concentration camp survivor, he could neither forget nor forgive, and should not be expected to do so."

How can any of us comment or make a judgement? As I have grown older I have come to realise more clearly the great value of both compassion and tolerance. To be able to be compassionate and tolerant we need constant inward renewal: in my own experience, our Quaker form of silent worship gives us this opportunity. When we are open to receive the Spirit, we can indeed as Advice 11 suggests, be given "the strength to go on with renewed courage".

CHAPTER 14

THE GROWTH OF FAITH: MY EXPERIENCE

AS I have already written, my mother came from a long line of Quaker families, on both sides; my father's parents joined the Society of Friends through the Adult School movement and he himself joined at the age of nineteen years. Thus I was born into a well-established Quaker family and no doubt absorbed much by 'osmosis'. But how did I become a "convinced Friend", a rather different matter? In the seventeenth century, to be "convinced" meant to be shown one's darkness by the Inward Light, the Light of Christ within. This certainly happened to me, for when life became difficult I had to face the fact that I was not the person I thought I was! How did a more honest faith come to be mine? After my four years at the Friends School in Saffron Walden which I left at sixteen years of age, I was a somewhat rebellious teenager, announcing to my parents that I was a Communist and atheist. Nevertheless a good deal of Quakerism and Quaker teaching rubbed off onto me. For example, on Sundays the whole school attended the Friends' Meeting in the town and though I may have scoffed with others, the silence had its influence. On Sunday evenings we had hymns and a talk from people well-known in the Quaker world, some of these speakers being very impressive in themselves and in what they had to say. In our Scripture classes we were introduced to the idea that the Bible was a compendium of history, legend and myth, as well as of spiritual truths. Nevertheless I was sure that since Quakers were "humble learners in the school of Christ" we should follow Jesus' teaching and example in the power of the Spirit. This led me at the outbreak of the Second World War, to join the Friends' Ambulance Unit. After a year I was seconded to the Friends' Relief Service to help look after evacuees from Hull. The warden of the hostel was a Seventh Day Adventist and sincere believer who put

96

her faith into practice daily. She once remarked to me that I had "all the right ideas, BUT ..."! I think she meant that my faith was more from the intellect than the heart, and she was right. This state of things continued, with my more or less conventional Quaker faith and attendance at Friends' Meetings for some years, until I was severely tested by the trials of my life.

From 1948, my husband was farming a small and remote farm in the North Yorkshire Dales while I, meanwhile had my hands full looking after a household of eight, the two of us, with two helpers and four young children, and another child expected. My husband became ill, (to the point where our doctor told me that "he would give him ten years if he didn't get out") - the farm was losing money, our cows on whose milk we depended for a living were afflicted by mastitis, with some deaths. The legacy from my parents, which we had hoped would put us to rights, had disappeared into a black hole. I came to realise that our situation was in no way viable. However, persuading my husband to see what was happening and the bleak outlook for our future proved exceedingly difficult, partly because he had invested so much emotionally in his dream, partly because his father had prophesied failure. I felt quite desperate and unable to do anything to alter our dire situation. I recall throwing myself down on the bed and saying aloud to God, "I'm at the end! I've been brought up to believe in you, so if you really do exist, please do something, as I cannot do any more!" Well, no clap of thunder, no still, small voice, but a faint sense of relief and support came to me. Gradually, things began to happen, in that the right people came into our lives and spoke the right words and were listened to by my husband. They sowed the seed which eventually bore fruit in our selling the farm and changing direction altogether. During this time, we rarely saw a newspaper but when shopping in the village (two miles away) I bought the "Northern Echo" for once. In the "Situations Vacant" section was an advert for a historian who was knowledgeable about farming, or a farmer with knowledge of history, to work at the Castle Museum in York on the new "Agricultural gallery"! My husband's chief asset for a possible career was his Oxford degree in History: and praise be, he got the job ...

Throughout the years of bringing up the family on a very small income, we had wonderful support from family and friends, and I often felt an inward blessing and sense of being sustained in difficult times, especially by Meeting for Worship. Later, when I found myself in another intractable situation, as the old Quakers used to say "the way opened", and the apparently impossible proved possible in an unexpected way.

When my faith falters, as it does: when I doubt the existence of a loving "God", and find the idea of divine "leadings" intellectually implausible, I have only to recall those testing times and the way in which difficulties were resolved, for my faith to be renewed afresh. Our Meetings for Worship are in my experience, times of spiritual recollection and refreshment when, as our *Advices* say:

> "in expectant waiting we may discover a deeper sense of God's presence".

Now that I have passed my Biblical "three score years and ten", I ask myself what have I learned on my spiritual journey so far? My experience has been in some respects, similar to those of many early Friends. As I turned the more to the Light, waiting in the Light in quietness, the more the Dark was revealed to me. As our first Quaker Advice says, "it is the Light which shows us our darkness and brings us to new Life". Before there could be any change, I had to be shown the shallowness of my Quaker faith: I had to reach a deeper realisation of my own blindness and failure to live up to my own aspirations, to my picture of myself as a "good Quaker". The extract from Jo Farrow in our *Quaker Faith and Practice* (26.29) speaks to my condition, then and now. She writes:

> "If we set ourselves on goodness as a personal goal, it means that we have to ignore or suppress all other parts of ourselves that do not fit into our ideal of goodness".

We need to recognise that all human beings are a mixture of the good and the bad in differing degrees. These proverbial lines (much quoted by my mother) speak truth:

> "There is so much bad in the best of us,
>
> And so much good in the worst of us,
>
> That it ill behoves any of us,
>
> To scorn the rest of us."

Paul Oestreicher put the same idea into more elegant language in an article in *The Friend* (5 September 1997):

> "We are all a complex mixture of light and darkness. In the world's scoundrels perhaps only God can see the light. In the world's saints, perhaps only God can see the darkness."

It is hard and demands courage and faith, to allow our Dark to rise into our full consciousness, so as to come to accept "the shadow" self within us. In my personal experience, this is a first step toward the "new life" of which the Advice speaks. As we feel impulses towards the good stirring within ourselves however faintly (sometimes even ignored), we are enabled to obey the first words of that same advice:

"Take heed, dear Friends, to the promptings of love and truth in your hearts. Trust them as the leadings of God ..."

When we open ourselves to the Light as individuals, and in oneness of spirit with other members of a Meeting for Worship we may hope to share with Robert Barclay his experience of being "secretly reached by the Life", and he goes on:

"so I become thus knit and united unto them (his fellow worshippers), hungering more and more after the increase of this power and life ...(Q.F. & P. Extract 19.21)

For me, sometimes the "leadings of God" are a slight inward pressure to say a particular word to someone or to take action of a practical kind. This chimes with the sense of being called to stand to give ministry in a Meeting for Worship. On some rare occasions there is almost a voice bidding me to take some action. If I am obedient (as I am not always) I have come to know the reason straightaway or at a later date; if I have been disobedient I have felt regret, bringing a sense of unworthiness.

There is also a different kind of experience of the "leadings of God" where the guidance and upholding does not seem to come from within us only. This sense of being led has been the experience of a countless number throughout the centuries. As I have described, when our family was in a dark place we were led out into new possibilities of life. If we turn inward, as George Fox repeatedly entreated his listeners to do, and seek there the Inner Light, the Inward Christ, we are strengthened in our dark times, in bearing ill-health, hardship, grief and all forms of suffering. If in our despair we cry out to God we may find the truth of the words:

"Behold, I make all things new!"

There are still mysteries which we find it hard to come to terms with, as we try to understand life. Prayer is not always answered in any way that we can grasp. We ask why so many truly good people have to bear so much pain? As the title of Rabbi Kushner's book asks *Why do Bad Things Happen to Good People?* We do not know the answer,

99

and this I have come to accept. How can I, with my small and finite brain understand the eternal, the infinite? We can meditate on the lives, the sufferings and the deaths of so many: Jesus, so filled with the Spirit, Gandhi, Martin Luther King and all the martyrs through the ages. Does spiritual renewal and deepened commitment to the good come from their deaths? As early as the eleventh century, Peter Abelard proclaimed his belief that this was the true meaning of Jesus' death on the cross, that we should be so inspired by his faithfulness to his "leadings" even to death, that our hearts would be fired by his example. This "Exemplar" theory appeals to me, whereas I find most theories of the "Atonement", such as the acceptance of Jesus' death as a vicarious propitiation for our sins, quite unacceptable. The story of the mythical phoenix arising from the flames of a consuming fire and the Resurrection stories of Jesus, all give us hope of new life arising after catastrophic events.

CHAPTER 15

MY EXPERIENCE AS A QUAKER

T HE men and women (of whom I have written in Part 1) whether they were seventeenth-century sufferers from intolerant or unjust laws or social reformers such as John Bellers and Elizabeth Fry, a relief worker such as API Cotterell or missionaries like my parents, have had to confront evil in both its personal and social manifestations. The Society of Friends has a long and honourable history in this respect; those lives described here represent many hundreds more, from the early days of the Society. All these Friends of past generations, having faced the dark in themselves, had a deep faith in their being led by God and empowered "to walk in the Light". This was the strength which gave them the ability to endure persecution, adverse criticism, hardship and danger. As with Robert Barclay the sources of their faith were found in "the secret power" present in their Meetings for Worship, as well as in their individual spirituality, their turning to what Fox described as "the Inward Teacher".

What of modern day British Friends? I do not, obviously cannot, give a full account of the present-day Society of Friends in general; I write only of my personal experience of being a Quaker and of Friends I have known of or have met. From my experience and observation, I conclude that if we wish to bring "light and love" to flow over every kind of "darkness and death", we need the deep faith and empowerment by the Spirit which is evident in so many of the lives of our Quaker forebears. We do not need to express our faith in exactly the same way, but the same attention to "leadings" and the rootedness in love, are essential. There are Friends among us today, however they are labelled, who have as deep a faith in the Inner Light and its universality as had earlier Friends; through the inspiration of that faith they are enabled to take practical and enduring action. As William Penn wrote:

"True godliness don't turn men out of the world but enables them to live better in it and excites their endeavours to mend it ..." (Q.F. & P. 24.02)

There are two especially remarkable people whom I recall from my schooldays; both gave talks in school at the Sunday evening meetings. I can still see in my mind's eye the tall figure of John Hoyland (1887-1957) a friend of my parents from their Woodbrooke days, a former Quaker missionary in India; afterwards, deeply troubled by the state of the unemployed during the Depression years of the 1930s, John Hoyland inspired groups of volunteers (Quakers and others from many countries) to join in Work Camps as a:

"way of self-identification with the poorest ... by means of hard work done at his side for his benefit". (Q.F. & P. 24.31)

Having heard his eloquent appeal at Saffron Walden, I volunteered to help in a mining area of high unemployment. Obviously my puny efforts in digging potatoes on their allotments had no effect on their general situation, but those weeks gave me some slight understanding of "how the other half lived" and some sympathy for their blighted lives, so that in later years I hotly rejected remarks about the laziness of the unemployed or that it was their own fault that they had found no work. In his old age when no longer able to be so physically active, John Hoyland became critical of some Friends who made no personal effort of a practical sort, but were arm-chair reformers. So he himself, started to make small Teddy bears which were sold for the benefit of the United Nations International Children's' Fund.

I remember also, again at school a visit from David Wills, a most impressive speaker. He told us of the Hawkspur Camp for troubled, sometimes delinquent boys, where they were helped to deal with their problems and their behaviour. The realisation dawned on me that most of those boys were not wicked, but were more sinned against than sinning, through their parents' treatment of them and the sort of environment in which they had grown up. Where children have had an over-strict upbringing ("spare the rod and spoil the child") or have been sexually and/or emotionally abused they often grow up with enormous anger within. This fund of anger all too often explodes in violence against others in their later life. From the life-stories which David Wills told us I began to appreciate the truth of the French saying:

"To know all is to understand all; to understand all is to forgive all."

I have known Friends who work as psychiatrists, counsellors or psychotherapists, social workers, teachers and some doctors who know from their training and experience of both the possible depths and heights which human beings can reach. This is also true for those Quakers involved in penal affairs, in prison visiting, or as prison chaplains, and for those engaged in conflict resolution, in mediation and Peace education at home and broad. Such Friends have to be realistic, knowing of the dark side in us, in all human beings but trusting that the "ocean of light and love" will flow over the "ocean of darkness and death".

This same faith was crucially important when Friends were called upon to be involved in war. Most of us have met or know of Friends who were conscientious objectors in the First and Second World Wars, as a refusal to take part in what they saw as evil and their attempt to demonstrate their belief in a better way. Some endured imprisonment, sometimes in "solitary". Walter Griffin, a former neighbour, when in solitary confinement told of his loud singing of carols in his cell to celebrate Christmas, partly so as to hear another human voice as the warder shouted at him that this was against the rules. John Brocklesby, a fellow member of Scunthorpe Meeting in the 1960s, was one of a small number of conscientious objectors who were taken from prison and put on a train to the battlefield in France during the 1914-1918 War. There they could be ordered "field punishment", a form of torture, or even be shot for disobeying military orders in the face of the enemy. This group was saved in the nick of time by a Parliamentary question. My former history teacher at Saffron Walden, Stanley King Beer talked to us of being ill-used when he refused to put on army uniform. Some conscientious objectors who suffered greatly in "solitary" or were abused became mentally or physically ill; a few died as a result of their treatment.

An alternative for those who refused to fight on grounds of conscience was to help to relieve the suffering caused by war. My father was one who worked with the "War Vics" (the Friends War Victims Relief Committee) for a short time during the First World War; my uncle as a doctor, also joined the "War Vics" which he left to join the British Navy. In the Second World War many Friends of call-up age joined the Friends Relief Service to help with evacuees, or to repair homes or to alleviate the miseries of refugees by feeding and caring for them and helping them to rebuild their lives. Others joined the Friends Ambulance Unit, as did my two brothers, and I myself for a short period. The F.A.U. members gave medical aid in hospitals for the wounded, they worked behind the lines for civilians; they sent F.A.U. sections to many parts of the world such as China, India, North Africa and the Middle East. A minority of members of the Society of Friends (an unknown number) fought in the army, navy or air force; whichever path their consciences impelled them to take, all were fighting evil as they saw it, in the one way or the other.

Just a moments' thought should remind us what we owe (Quakers and pacifists in particular) to the men and women of the armed forces during the Second World War. The Royal Navy ships and submarines secured our food and supplies; the RAF held off some of the bombers and also helped to prevent a German invasion; the anti-aircraft batteries and the army all played their part with great courage.

Had it been otherwise, had Nazi Germany invaded and occupied Britain, it does not take much imagination to realise the likely fate of for example, any who helped Jews or who took action against a Nazi-imposed règime!

Towards the end of the Second World War atomic bombs were dropped on Hiroshima and Nagasaki; warfare was changed for ever; former assumptions about the inevitable continuation of life on this planet were destroyed. Years later, the accident at Chernobyl and consequent far-flung pollution by radioactivity has strengthened this realisation. Many Quakers became active in the Campaign for Nuclear Disarmament: some Quaker women supported the camps at Greenham Common. Some Friends, with others, came to believe that in paying for the production of nuclear weapons through our taxes was an involvement with evil. This issue was taken up by the Society of Friends, which as employers decided to withhold 12% of the tax due from thirty-three of their employees, a matter of conscience for those members of staff. (This was the percentage of tax, it was calculated would be spent on military preparations.) The decision resulted in the two Clerks of Meeting for Sufferings, Beryl Hibbs and Maisie Birmingham, being summoned to appear before the Mayor's and City of London County Court on January 22 1985. This was a testing of the law, and when the case was lost, the Society took no further action but allowed the officers of the Inland Revenue to collect what was legally due.

Some individual Friends up and down the country took similar action to divert or withhold a proportion of their Income Tax, and I was one of those. It had taken me about seven years to move on from my earlier sense that I could not in honesty, share in any way in the

Friends' Peace Testimony; I came to realise that we are not to wait till we are perfect ourselves before we act against evil. In those intervening years I had come to forgive others involved with me and had accepted a sense of forgiveness for myself from what I can only call God. First, I joined the Peace Tax Campaign in its efforts to change the law so as to allow for tax diversion from war preparations to peaceful purposes; this campaign is ongoing in the twenty-first century.

I also joined with Quakers and other like-minded people in the activities of Peace Action Durham. A small group, mostly of Friends met for a regular silent vigil in Durham market-place beneath a banner of the "Peace Prayer" held aloft. Some members of my Meeting, member of Peace Action Durham and Quaker Peace and Service from Friends House gave me great support in my attempt to divert a proportion of my Income Tax from military to peaceful purposes. This demanded two court appearances for which there was much publicity in the local media, a notoriety which I did not care for. It was strange to step off a train at the railway station to see a newspaper billboard with "Durham Gran in Tax Protest" displayed! Eventually the sum demanded was "garnisheed" from my bank account, against the wishes of my bank manager. After that episode the Inland Revenue arranged to take all I might owe directly at source from my pension. Some time after I had left Durham I received one last bill from the Inland Revenue, which unlike the heroic Quaker couple, the Windsors, I paid. It seemed to me that such protests are but symbolic gestures and could not succeed, but at least make some people think more deeply about the issues of war and peace. Since we live in a democracy, I now think the Peace Tax Campaign is working along the right lines in trying to persuade enough Members of Parliament to vote for a change in the law so that those who wish may pay part of their tax towards projects for the building of peace in the world.

CHAPTER 16

"DARKNESS AND DEATH": "LIGHT AND LOVE"

As time has passed and the twenty-first century opens before us, the people of Europe have as far as possible, put the difficult years of the Second World War and the Cold War behind them. Generally speaking, except for those families imprisoned on "sink estates" or in rural poverty, most of us have become more affluent, more comfortable and under less pressure; it is easier then to turn a blind eye to the dark things in the world and to repress and deny any dark feelings in ourselves. Yet as Jo Farrow has pointed out (Q.F. & P. Extract 26.29) it was not until George Fox accepted his own inner dark, accepted that he could be "bestial, murderous or depraved" that he found "a more liberating truth at the heart of himself". We are not the best selves we could be, we are not able to bring "light and love" to others, if we have become "healthy-minded", "sweetness and light" Friends! For some it has been tempting to join a pacifist Society where there will be, it is hoped, peaceable and friendly people; this is especially likely if you are a person who is afraid of, even one who denies, your angry and aggressive feelings. Of course there have been times when I too, have acted the part of a peaceable and loving person when my true emotions were different. We tend to escape from this side of ourselves when possible. I remember a Quaker study circle of which I was a member, where we were asked to consider our "Inner Dark"; however, the facilitator said that this was "too depressing", so we went on to discuss the "Inner Light". Advice number 11 asks if we are "evading unpalatable truths"? We may evade unpalatable truths not only about ourselves, but about the world, looking only for the silver lining of every cloud, denying the cloud itself, however black and storm-laden it might be.

I have still a recollection from just before the Second World War which illustrates this point. In the late 1930s Friends of varying degrees of "weightiness" spoke at gatherings throughout the country on the possible ways of avoiding war with Germany which many observers of the international scene saw as inevitable after the failure of the League of Nations to deal effectively with Japan's invasion of Manchuria and Italy's invasion of Abyssinia. The Friend who addressed us at the lecture I attended gave a heartfelt and appreciative account of the many German artists, scholars, philosophers, composers, musicians and scientists of the past few hundred years. All true of course: but this was the Nazi time, with Hitler making his threats of Germany "uber alles", and news coming through of the persecution of the Jews. The peroration left me amazed, hardly believing what my ears were hearing, for the speaker concluded "we must build on all the good of the past and remember, too" the voice rising "that both Hitler and Goering are vegetarians!" These final words of the lecture were the only reference to the Nazis. At first I thought this was some sort of joke, but soon realised it was not. I had recently left the Friends School, Saffron Walden where there were a number of Jewish refugee children. The seniors knew of the aims of Adolf Hitler as expressed by *Mein Kampf* from our remarkable history teacher, Stanley King Beer. A Sunday evening talk by Gwen Catchpool had told us something of the heroic work of the Friends' Germany Emergency Committee in helping Jews and anti-Nazi Germans.   Here Friends were recognising and confronting an evil, and taking action to prevent the consequences of evil deeds, as far as possible for a small Society.

We are not always so honest and forthright in our condemnation of wickedness, nor in our resultant actions. When I spent a term at Woodbrooke I got to know Farid Esack, a member of the African National Congress from South Africa. Farid has a great respect for the Society of Friends and acknowledges his debt to what he learned at Woodbrooke in many aspects of his life. Nevertheless, he found it so puzzling that some Quakers, in the interest of their impartiality, thought it right to keep silent in the face of great wrong - neither to confront nor to condemn. He is not happy with this attitude which he found among some Friends both inside and outside Woodbrooke. In 1993 he spoke honestly and movingly of his thoughts and feelings:

> "Quakerism has rubbed off onto me, at least Woodbrooke and Quakerism. Tread carefully. Never tread on people's toes. Be very, very careful. This lethal combination of that of God in everyone and English politeness. It has destroyed for me so

much authenticity, so much of what is genuinely human to be angry, to have feelings, to be frustrated, to laugh and to cry and to be annoyed. So often in the struggle to avoid treading on people's toes decisions aren't made."

He went on to say that he felt that in so doing we:

"are sacrificing our own spirit, our own humanness and in this dealing with people who walk over us, diminishing our own dignity ..."

These words struck home to me because in my own life I have at times when faced by domineering persons "bent over backwards to accommodate other people" and in so doing, have condoned wrong actions. Looking back I can see my behaviour was aimed sometimes at peace-keeping, at other times it was cowardice.

"Quakers" said Farid:

"are nice people. All the Quakers are nice people. Having said this, I don't think it's nice to be nice. I have serious problems with niceness".

The same unease is expressed in an article in the *Friends' Journal* (December 1995) by H. Otto Dahlke of Richmond Meeting, Virginia, USA:

"To be nice, we are inclined to believe, is a virtue. It is a pretty word with a sweet array of charming synonyms. How different from a defiant word like 'confrontation'! 'Nice' suggests a sort of reasonableness, a no-offence to anybody quality. 'Agreement' is so much more cosy than 'disagreement'. Better to be affable than critical; better to be well-mannered and diplomatic than forthright and rough."

However, to be "forthright" and outspoken is not always wise, may even be counter-productive, as William Sewell found in his many years in China, and as Quaker Peace and Service workers in trouble spots in the world today have found by experience. Nevertheless Otto Dahlke is correct in contrasting the forthrightness of speech and fierce denunciations of wickedness made by the prophets of the Old Testament, by Jesus himself and George Fox and early Friends, too, with our present-day milder manner of speech; we believe it is better not to offend others.

Is it fear of what may be discovered buried in ourselves, the fear that we may be unable to deal with what might be revealed which makes us cover up, keep to surface politeness, and to keep quiet when we should speak? I well remember an incident from years ago; I was at a Monthly Meeting where some indignation was expressed because of accusations of malpractice made by a particular Friend. There was unease and ill-feeling in the meeting which could be sensed though little was expressed openly; some of the office-holders threatened to resign. Rather suddenly the Friend who had raised objections to certain actions of the Monthly Meeting left the area. The matters he had raised seemed to me to need to be addressed, as some of his points in my view, were valid. There was no further discussion, however, and the Friends who had threatened to resign from office, one of whom had expressed the intention of resigning from the Society of Friends altogether, withdrew these threats. Different Friends stood up and said in effect, that everything should return to how things were before. The problems and the angry feelings aroused were simply "brushed under the carpet". The situation demanded that one of those present should challenge and confront the assumption that this was an appropriate resolution, but nobody did so; with hindsight, I should have plucked up the courage to re-open the question, but, feeling nervous and not considering myself to be a sufficiently "weighty" Friend, I kept silent. Otto Dalhke concluded his article with these words:

> "Confrontation does not necessarily mean being hateful; we should and can speak the truth in love as well as in justice ... the niceness syndrome stands in the way of facing squarely the fact of evil in the world".

Not only in the world, but perhaps "the niceness syndrome" among Quakers prevents us from seeing the "shadow" side of the Society of Friends as a body. Do we, as a Society, evade "unpalatable truths"? Beth Allen of Quaker Home Service touched on this negative side in a talk she gave to Woodbrooke in 1998; in correspondence following her talk she wrote:

> "I am increasingly aware of the shadow side of the Society of Friends (not just Britain Yearly Meeting). We also have a tendency to avoid conflict and to ignore it in the name of peace."

Beth Allen concluded her letter to me by quoting from the prophet Jeremiah:

> "They have healed the hurt of my people, lightly saying 'Peace, peace when there is no peace'". (Jer.6.14)

Nevertheless she believes that "the shadow, the darkness, is also a source of our creative energy". (I should prefer to say "can be" rather than "is the source of our creative energy".) Do not seeds have to lie hidden in darkness before growing towards the light and emerging as new green shoots of life?

Conflict is an inescapable part of life and Friends are now addressing the problems raised by conflict, both at gatherings at Woodbrooke and, for example, at the Britain Yearly Meeting of May 2000. As Mary Lou Leavitt has pointed out (Q.F. & P. Extract 20.71) conflict need not always become destructive, need not be part of "darkness and death". She gives us guidelines for dealing with conflict creatively; she begins with the observation that "a world where we are all agreed with one another would be incredibly boring" Mary Lou believes that we can even change and grow spiritually through conflict; this is sometimes essential before "real change - either political or personal can happen". She offers three keys, three skills which she has found helpful in her own life:

> "The first skill is *naming*: being clear and honest about the problem as I see it, stating what I see and how I feel about it."

No hiding behind phrases such as "surely it is obvious that", but owning up to our own views and feelings.

> Such a skill is dangerous. It can feel - indeed, it can be - confrontational. It feels like stirring up trouble where there wasn't any problem. It needs to be done carefully, caringly, with love, in language we hope others can hear. We need to seek tactfully the best time to do it. But it needs to be done.

> The second skill is the skill of *listening*: listening not just to the words, but to the feelings and needs behind the words. It takes a great deal of time and energy to listen well. It's a kind of weaving: reflecting back, asking for clarification, asking for time in turn to be listened to, being truly open to what we're hearing (even if it hurts), being open to the possibility that we might ourselves be changed by what we hear.

> The third skill is the skill of *letting go*: I don't mean that in the sense of giving up, lying down and inviting people to walk all over us, but acknowledging the possibility that there may be other solutions to this conflict than the ones we've thought of yet; letting the imagination in - making room for the Spirit. We need to let go of our own will - not so as to surrender to another's, but so as to look together for God's solution. It's a question of finding ways to let go of our commitment to opposition and separation, of letting ourselves be opened to our connectedness as human beings.

If we are to do any of these things well - naming, listening, letting go - we need to have learned to trust that of God in ourselves and that of God in those trapped on all sides of the conflict with us. And to do that well, I find I need to be centred, rooted, practised in waiting on God. That rootedness is both a gift and a discipline, something we can cultivate and build on by acknowledging it every day."

Mary Lou Leavitt, 1986 (Q.F. & P. 20.71)

If we are "centred, rooted, practised in waiting on God" in our daily lives we shall be able to do great things, "deeds of love" as Patricia Loring writes in her Introduction to *Listening Spirituality*; and she continues with the observation that the converse is also true:

"Activity that does not take time to find its source and grounding in prayer, worship and divine leading becomes dry, exhausting and exasperating - or an exercise in power".

We know that, unlike the Friends whose lives I describe in Part 1 we do not always take time, are not always so focussed in our daily lives. Sometimes we are undisciplined, lazy or rebellious and like Paul have to admit that "the spirit is willing but the flesh is weak". Sometimes we share Paul's darker experience, "the good I would I do not, the evil that I would not, I find that I have done". The turning away from the leadings of the Spirit, this estrangement from God is what orthodox Christians call "sin"; but we Quakers seem to have no word for it. We speak and write of the Inner Light, rarely of its opposite within ourselves or in others. No child brought up in a Quaker family is taught to say the Heidelberg Catechism, which my Dutch friend had to learn:

"What causes the sinfulness of men?

The fall of Adam and Eve

Since then we are incapable of any good

And inclined to all evil."

She has joined the Society of Friends and must find such a change a lifting of the heart! Such teaching is at one extreme; but at times, from the seventeenth century onward, Friends have made extreme statements too. About twenty years ago a Friends Home Service Committee leaflet entitled "What Friends Believe" claimed that "Friends believe that we are all born good". Is this the lingering of the seventeenth-century Quaker belief in the possibility of reaching

111

perfection in this life? I do not see how such beliefs can be held in all honesty; I know that I am not totally good; and I have never met anyone totally without faults of any kind. If "we are all born good", what has gone wrong? If we are all born good, how do we account for the Holocaust, for Ruanda, for Kosovo, for a century of wars?

Since we are "born in the image of God"; how is it that we ignore or even turn away from "the promptings of love and truth in our hearts? I have searched for an answer to this question from the writings of Anglicans, Roman Catholics, Jews and Quakers; they all conclude that human beings have a choice in the way that we live, for we have been given Free Will. Unless we are to be automata, forced by our nature to choose to live good lives, we must be able to choose either good or evil, and abide by the consequences of our choice of action. Many of the orthodox Christian theologians teach that evil is inevitable in a "fallen world", following on from the "Original Sin" of Adam and Eve's disobedience to God in the paradise of the Garden of Eden. No former "Golden Age" of humanity, no trace of any such garden of perfection has ever been discovered by historians or archaeologists, for this is a mythical story which yet has meaning for us today.

Very few Friends of Britain Yearly Meeting would accept the story of Adam and Eve as an explanation; many of us, and I include myself would prefer the evolutionary teaching, that the Genesis story is a myth picturing our creation by God, and an attempt to explain our turning to the Dark instead of to the Light. The story tells of the first glimmerings of an understanding of the moral choice between good and evil as experienced by our remote ancestors. Not a "Fall", but morally, a step up! I believe that we humans are born with the potentiality for both good and evil, and have the power to make our choice of action.

I know of no explanation convincing to me, for the existence of evil and suffering; I suspect we have to live with our doubts and our unresolved questions. There are some theories which seem to me to have truth in them. Alice Miller, the Swiss psychiatrist is convinced by her work with patients and her own life-experience, that almost all of the destructiveness, abuse and violence in the world results from insensitive or cruel methods of child-rearing suffered by their perpetrators. However, Alice Miller appears to disregard other possible causes of violent behaviour, for example sibling jealousy, which in an extreme form can lead to a Cain and Abel situation. She also disregards the thirst for justice in all human beings, which when thwarted can lead to violence; there is also the overwhelming desire for revenge for injustice suffered, or for personal injury received. Nor does she mention the basic instinct for survival in us all, survival of self, of family, of tribe. I well recall, now with some sense of shame, how I was determined to have my baby admitted to the Children's Hospital where there was only one bed available; I felt little sympathy for the mother and baby who were turned away! On TV News bulletins of the relief effort in Mozambique after the floods and famine there, we saw the strongest ones take food parcels away from the weaker ones, often running off, exultant. The commentators remarked that we were watching an example of the "survival of the fittest". We see the same "survival mode" in people born and brought up in poor, slum areas, whether in the countryside or in cities. I really doubt whether their children grow up with the possibility of making free choices between good and evil actions.

We need to heed the words of Hugh Barbour in his history of Friends, *The Quakers in Puritan England*. He is telling us that we have to deal with our own inner demons before we can become whole, become integrated personalities. Until we then have respect for ourselves we cannot love or respect or help others at a spiritual level. Where he writes of the Quakers of the present day, he concludes that we have to face these questions:

> "Modern Quakers who show a radical, world-changing spirit are sometimes confused or shallow in their vision of the evil they are fighting. Their fierce, inner fight may not yet be won and so is projected crookedly on the world ... but the heart of Quakerism was the freedom of those confidently dependent on the Spirit; only those who have known such power can confidently lead the Lamb's War ... Early Quakerism will be reborn in our time only when personal understanding of the depth of evil (with a precision drawn from psychology and theology) can be combined with the free power of the Spirit of God to overcome it."

Some American Friends have made an attempt to come to "a personal understanding of the depth of evil"; fifty-one Quakers from twenty-four Yearly Meetings, members of Friends' United Meeting, Friends' General Conference, the Evangelical Friends' Alliance and Independent Yearly Meetings, met together for a "Consultation on Overcoming Sin and Evil". The Introduction to the Report makes clear that:

"although no-one expected to resolve the issue, at least Friends were forthright in sharing and dialoguing about an important topic which they normally try to avoid".

In spite of the very different beliefs and viewpoints of this group of Friends, their conclusions are enheartening. Rufus Jones is quoted on our Quaker forebears:

"They moved straight against the glaring and invisible evil with a remarkable quality of purity".

The lives I describe in Part 1 are witness to that statement. Charles Thomas writes in the same report:

"Friends have inherited a principle of overcoming evil in themselves and in society."

This is not:

"skin-deep piety ... but a genuine holiness which answers the call of the Spirit, the Light of Christ, the Truth that is God. Evil can be overcome by good. It will not be overcome in any other way ... all of which is love at work ... There is no other way."

This truth was illuminated for me and I am sure for many others when The Quaker Festival Orchestra and Chorus presented Francis Grier's *Embracing the Tiger* in the Birmingham Symphony Hall. This is described as a "choral drama of courage, darkness and transformation" and:

"sings those moments when spontaneous human courage boldly arrests and transforms the tiger power of oppression and destruction".

We hear the story of Amrita Devi whose courage in facing evil led to her sacrificial death and to victory for her cause. The willingness to love and to suffer rather than to cause suffering to others is the theme of the overcoming of evil from the death of Jesus to the present day. This is for me, the meaning of our Quaker Peace Testimony; we can be in no doubt that in time of war or when facing violence, sacrificial death might well be the outcome of putting our Peace Testimony into practice. My understanding of the "Cross" is that it is for us to, as it were, absorb evil done to us into ourselves and not to do evil again in return but to react in a loving spirit, being willing to forgive, and in hope of reconciliation. This demands a quality of saintliness, from us, a quality we may have only if we walk in the Light, paying attention day by day to the Inward Christ. Sometimes I want to emulate Augustine's:

"Make me good, but not yet, oh Lord! for Saintliness feels to be a daunting prospect, almost impossibly demanding."

This Celtic Canticle and Blessing speaks to me, bearing in mind that by "Christ" I understand what is meant is the spirit which filled Jesus and is in us all in lesser measure:

"Christ as a light illumine and guide me
Christ as a shield o'ershadow me: Christ under me
Christ over me
Christ beside me on my left and on my right.
This day be within and without me
Lowly and meek yet all-powerful
Be in each to whom I speak
In the mouth of each who speaks to me,
This day be within and without me.
Christ the light illumine me.

May the peace of the Lord Christ go with you
    wherever he may send you.
May He guide you through the wilderness,
    protect you through the storm,
May He bring you home rejoicing
    at the wonders He has shown you,
May He bring you home rejoicing
    once again into our doors.

George Fox's message is one of rejoicing, for in his "opening", his vision, he saw that the love of God for us would overcome all evil, the "infinite ocean of light and love" flowing "over the ocean of darkness and death":

"Sing and rejoice, ye children of the Day and of the Light; for the Lord is at work in this thick night of Darkness that may be felt; and Truth doth flourish as the rose, and the lilies do grow among the thorns, and the plants atop of the hills, and upon them the lambs do skip and play. And never heed the tempests nor the storms, floods nor rains, for the Seed Christ is over all and doth reign, so be of good faith and valiant for the Truth."

Quaker Faith and Practice, Extract 20.23.

GENERAL BIBLIOGRAPHY

Hugh Barbour: *The Quakers in Puritan England*, Yale University Press, New Haven, Coun., 1964.

H.S. Barbour & A.O. Roberts, Eds.: *Early Quaker Writings* (1650-1700), Eerdman, Grand Rapids, Mich., 1973.

The Bible: The Authorised Version of 1611 (King James), Oxford University Press, 1897 (my father's copy); The Revised Standard Version, British and Foreign Bible Society, 1979.

Marcus Borg: *Meeting JESUS AGAIN for the First Time*, Harper, San Francisco, 1995.

Jocelyn Burnell: *Broken for Life*, Swarthmore Lecture 1989, Quaker Home Service.

Etienne Charpentier: *How to Read the New Testament*, and *How to Read the Old Testament*, SCM Press Ltd., London, 1981.

John Cowburn, S.J.: *Shadows and the Dark*, SCM Press, 1979.

Ben P. Dandelion: *A Sociological Analysis of The Theology of Quakers*, Edwin Mellen, 1996.

Francis Dewar: *Live for a Change*, Darton, Longman & Todd, (Revised edition), 1999.

Austin Farrer: *Love Almighty and Ills Unlimited*, Collins, 1962.

Jo Farrow: *The World in My Heart*, Q.H.S., 1990.

Matthew Fox: *Original Blessing*, Bear & Co., Santa Fe, New Mexico, U.S.A., 1983.

Harvey Gillman: *A Light that is Shining*, Quaker Home Service, 1997.

Mollie Grubb (now Hooper): *Quakers Observed in Prose & Verse*, Sessions, York, 1993.

Douglas Gwyn: *Apocalypse of the Word: The Life & Message of George Fox (1624-1691)*, Friends United Press, Richmond, Indiana, U.S.A., 1984.

Brian Hebblewhite: *Evil, Suffering & Religion*, Sheldon Press, London, 1979.

Alistair Heron: *Quakers in Britain: a Century of Change (1895-1995)*, Curlew Graphics, 1995.

John Hick: *Evil and the God of Love*, Macmillan, London, 1966.

William James: *The Varieties of Religious Experience*, Longmans, Green & Co., London, 1907.

Diana Lampen: *Trouble Valley: The Door of Hope: Darkness & Light in the Spiritual Journey*, Friends Fellowship of Healing, No. 14, 1995.

John Lampen: *Mending Hurts*, Swarthmore Lecture, Quaker Home Service, 1987.

Alison Leonard: *Telling our Stories*, Darton, Longman & Todd, London, 1995.

Patricia Loring: *Listening Spirituality*, Vols. I & II, Openings Press, Washington Grove, M.D., U.S.A., 1999.

Vera Massey: *The Clouded Quaker Star*: James Nayler, Sessions, York, England, with Friends United Press, Richmond, Indiana, U.S.A., 1999.

Alice Miller: *For Your Own Good: the Roots of Violence in Child-Rearing*, Virago, London, 1983.

Alice Miller: *Banished Knowledge*, Virago, London, 1991.

Geoffrey Nuttall: *The Holy Spirit in Puritan Faith and Experience*, Blackwell, Oxford, 1946.

John Punshon: *Testimony & Tradition*, Swarthmore Lecture 1990, Quaker Home Service.

John Punshon: *Portrait in Grey: a Short History of the Quakers*, Quaker Home Service, 1984.

Quaker Faith & Practice: the Book of Christian Discipline of the Yearly Meeting of the Religious Society of Friends (Quakers) in Britain. Approved at Yearly Meeting, 1994. Published by the Yearly Meeting of the Religious Society of Friends (Quakers) in Britain, 1995.

Reginald Reynolds: *The Wisdom of John Woolman*, Friends Home Service Committee, London 1948.

Alan Richardson (Ed.): *A Theological Word Book of the Bible*, SCM Press Ltd., 1957.

Adrian B. Smith: *The God Shift*, New Millennium, London, 1996.

Thich Nhat Hanh: *The Miracle of Mindfulness*, Rider, London, 1991.

Jack H. Wallis: *Jung & the Quaker Way*, ed. Emily Miles, Quaker Home Service, 1999.

Alex Wildwood: *A Faith to Call Our Own*, Swarthmore Lecture, Quaker Home Service, 1999.

PRIMARY SOURCES

George Fox: *The Journal*, ed. Nigel Smith, Penguin, London, 1999.

This I Affirm statements of personal faith, ed. Harvey Gillman, Quaker Home Service, 1999.

John Woolman, *Journal* with Introduction by John Greenleaf Whittier, Headley Bros., London & Ashford, Kent, 1871.